RESOURCE GUIDE
For
WOMEN'S
MINISTRY

REVISED & UPDATED

Linda McGinn Waterman

BROADMAN
&HOLMAN
PUBLISHERS

NASHVILLE, TENNESSEE

10-digit ISBN: 080543187X
13-digit ISBN: 9780805431872

Published by Broadman & Holman Publishers,
Nashville, Tennessee

Dewey Decimal Classification: 248.843
Subject Heading: WOMEN–RELIGIOUS LIFE \
CHURCH WORK WITH WOMEN

Unless otherwise noted, Scripture quotations are from the
Holy Bible, New International Version, copyright © 1973,
1978, 1984 by International Bible Society. Other versions
used: NASB, the New American Standard Bible, © the
Lockman Foundation, 1960, 1962, 1963, 1968, 1971, 1972,
1973, 1975, 1977; used by permission; RSV, the Revised
Standard Version of the Bible, copyrighted 1946, 1952,
© 1971, 1973; TLB, The Living Bible, copyright © Tyndale
House Publishers, Wheaton, Ill., 1971, used by permission;
and KJV, King James Version.

1 2 3 4 5 6 7 8   10 09 08 07 06 05

To my precious husband
Reen D. Waterman Jr.
whose love and encouragement
keeps me writing and T. R. Hollingsworth, author, teacher,
editor, conference speaker, and best of all my mother

Both of whom inspire me to fully pursue the good
works God prepared for me to accomplish before the
foundations of the earth.

May he be glorified!

CONTENTS

ACKNOWLEDGMENTS

I WANT TO THANK Elisabeth Elliot and Ruth Bell Graham for their role as mentors in my life. I thank Elisabeth for her example of uncompromising faith and Ruth for her example of joyful perseverance.

I am particularly grateful to the many women who shared their ideas and experiences in these pages, hoping to equip other women to be used by God for his glory, honor, and praise.

INTRODUCTION

THE CHILDREN SCATTERED, and I was about to dip my hands into the warm, soapy dishwater when the telephone rang.

"Linda," my friend Fran said. "You'll never guess who just called." I could tell from her voice that she was excited.

"Who?" I asked.

"You remember that I mentioned Beth Knighton, who works for MAP International. She's coming by for a visit. Would you like to come and meet her?" Fran asked.

I knew about MAP International through Fran and her husband Jim, who have been supporting the organization financially for years. To meet Beth Knighton was a special privilege since she was experienced in ministering to women in the United States and abroad. Ministry to women recently became one of my greatest interests as I recognized God's love for women portrayed in the Bible.

As I sat in Fran's cozy den that afternoon warmed by the crackling fire, I listened to Beth's story and silently thanked God for providing this unique opportunity.

Beth, a tall woman in her late fifties with slightly graying hair and a vibrant smile, spoke of the rich and full life she and Ray, her husband, had experienced in their marriage and their work, first with the Christian Medical Society and then in the development of MAP.

She spoke of both good times and bad, but her obvious joy in the work was contagious. I wanted to learn more.

As I listened, I thought about the rewards found in doing God's work when we yield ourselves to his will and plan for our lives. He uses us to touch the hearts of others. Beth gave me a key definition that afternoon as she spoke of ministry to women. She began by quoting the words in the Bible spoken to Jesus by an expert in the law (Luke 10:25–29):

> *"Teacher," he asked, "what must I do to inherit eternal life?"*
>
> *"What is written in the Law?" he [Jesus] replied. "How do you read it?"*
>
> *He answered: "'Love the Lord your God with all your heart and with all your soul and with all your strength and with all your mind'; and, 'Love your neighbor as yourself.'"*
>
> *"You have answered correctly," Jesus replied. "Do this and you will live."*
>
> *But he wanted to justify himself, so he asked Jesus, "And who is my neighbor?"*

Jesus then continued with the parable of the good Samaritan. Beth and the people of MAP International used this biblical passage to define *neighbor*. Beth's definition of *neighbor* was this: "My *neighbor* is any person who has a need which I have the ability to meet."

Asking, "Who is my neighbor?" can serve to guide and direct us as we desire to discover God's ministry for our lives as women.

I wrote the above words more than a decade ago. Now as I consider updating and revising this book, I realize I have so much more to share with you, my readers. God has taught me more about ministry to women in these ten plus years, and it is with great joy I share the story of lives touched and hearts changed, the narrative of truth sought and insight discovered.

Resource Guide for Women's Ministry offers you practical and creative ideas for leading prayer groups, using your home in a hospitality ministry, beginning outreach programs, forming fellowship support groups, and much more. May you discover the ministry God has for you, and may his purposes be accomplished through you for his glory.

"For we are God's workmanship, created in Christ Jesus to do good works, which God prepared in advance for us to do" (Eph. 2:10).

Chapter 1

PERSONAL INVENTORY AND PREPARATIONS

HAVE YOU BEEN ASKED to plan a program for the women in your church? Has your youngest child left to begin kindergarten, and you are asking the Lord how he wants you to use these free hours? Are you singled out by others for leadership even though you try to stay "behind the scenes"? God may be encouraging you to step out in new areas of your life, perhaps to develop a specific ministry chosen by God for you alone.

As you consider this possibility, you may be asking yourself, "Am I ready?" You may wonder, *How can anyone prepare to do the work of God?* Yet the dictionary defines *ministry* as "the act of ministering or serving." By daily serving your family, friends, and community, you may be preparing yourself to respond to God's call.

Jesus is our greatest example of service. In Philippians 2:6–7 we are told that our attitudes should be shaped by Jesus Christ.

Who [Jesus], being in very nature God, did not consider equality with God something to be grasped, but made himself nothing, taking the very nature of a servant, being made in human likeness.

What were the qualities Jesus displayed? In Philippians 2:3–4 we read, "Do nothing out of selfish ambition or vain conceit, but in humility consider others better than yourselves. Each of you should look not to your own interests, but also to the interests of others."

Few of us feel qualified or worthy to lead others. Because we are acutely aware of our own inadequacies, we feel someone else could do a better job. However, through the unique experiences, circumstances, and events of our lives, God has equipped us to minister to others. And thankfully, by his Spirit living in us, he uses us as his instruments to personally complete his work. We are not left alone.

As Beth Knighton stated, "Anyone who has a need that God has equipped me to meet is my neighbor." This is true. Does that mean we are to try to meet the needs of every person we meet? That would be impossible. When God reveals a person's need to us, he will give us either the ability to meet it or the insight to contact another person who is capable of meeting that specific need. A friend may come to me about financial problems, and I may not have the resources to help. But I may recommend another believer who has the expertise, or I may call on the local church body for help.

Jesus says, "Love your neighbor as yourself" (Luke 10:27), so the privilege of ministry is ours. You may wonder how God prepares us for ministry. Our ability may come through difficult life experiences. Have you been through a crisis with a teenager? Have you overcome financial struggles? Do you remember how you handled the busy hours of young motherhood or the loneliness of widowhood? God comforts and teaches us during these difficult periods of life so that we can reach out and comfort others. We can praise God "who comforts us in all our troubles, so that we can comfort those in any trouble with the comfort we ourselves have received from God" (2 Cor. 1:4).

Many times we are equipped with a particular talent or skill for service that is different from others. I remember Myrna Alexander's testimony. A pastor's wife and author of several women's Bible study books, she spoke at a women's luncheon I attended and told the story of a woman named Emily.

Emily felt deeply hurt and frustrated because she thought she had no gift to offer God. One day she shared her distress with Myrna whose reply was simple. She turned to Emily and asked, "What do you really like to do?"

Emily paused to think for a moment before answering, "Sewing, I guess. Sewing is one thing I really enjoy."

Myrna smiled, "Then, Emily," she said, "Sew. Sew for God's glory! Use this skill to minister to Christ's body, his church."

Emily left Myrna's home that day and prayerfully considered the suggestion. Later a beaming Emily approached Myrna after a church service. "I am going to sew for Jesus!" she said, "I've invited several young mothers to meet with me each week. I plan to teach them to sew while we have a time of Christian fellowship and encouragement."

God used Emily's gifts and skills for his glory. What are the gifts and skills he has assigned you? What experiences has God used to comfort and teach you that you can share with others? Before we can effectively reach out and serve others, it is helpful to ask ourselves certain important questions. Are you ready to search for the special ministry God equipped you to fulfill? Take time to consider and complete the following Personal Inventory Questionnaire that is divided into three parts.

In the first part of the questionnaire, biblical passages and questions are provided to help you examine your heart to see if you are developing into the woman God intends you to be. Though we are all imperfect, God provides goals and aspirations in his Word that give us direction as we seek to become women he can use for his glory. The next questions are offered to help you identify your God-given talents, skills, and abilities. Finally, you will be provided methods for identifying the needs of others and for discovering ways you can personally meet those needs. Reflect and enjoy this time as you consider God's work and plan for your life.

Personal Inventory Questionnaire

Have you put your hope in God by placing your faith in the Lord Jesus Christ, trusting him with your life?

- Have you accepted Jesus' complete and total forgiveness so you are free to move forward in your desire to fulfill his purposes for your life? Are there any unresolved areas of your life where you still need to ask for forgiveness and find restoration? Prayerfully ask the Lord Jesus to reveal these to you.

- Ask yourself where you now stand in your relationship with the Lord. Although we all are in the process of growing, do you personally desire to be all that God created you to be?

Paul challenges us, "'Love your neighbor as yourself.' Love does no harm to its neighbor. Therefore love is the fulfillment of the law. And do this, understanding the present time. The hour has come for you to wake up from your slumber, because our salvation is nearer now than when we first believed. The night is nearly over; the day is almost here. . . . Clothe yourselves with the Lord Jesus Christ, and do not think about how to gratify the desires of the sinful nature" (Rom. 13:9–12, 14).

Have you sought the inner beauty described in the following passage?

Peter states, "Your beauty should not come from outward adornment. . . . Instead it should be that of your inner self, the unfading beauty of a gentle and quiet spirit, which is of great worth in God's sight. For this is the way the holy women of the past who put their hope in God used to make themselves beautiful" (1 Pet. 3:3–5).

Have you sought the following qualities attesting to your faith in the Lord Jesus and his Word?

1. *Dignity*–Does your behavior and reputation honor the Lord?

2. *Integrity*–Do you control your tongue and seek to be truthful?

3. *Temperate*—Do you seek to be moderate in action and speech?

In 1 Timothy 3:11, we find the following guidance. "Women must likewise be dignified, not malicious gossips, but temperate, faithful in all things" (NASB).

If married, have you considered your family's feelings? Will your children receive the time and concern they need? Is your husband willing to support you as you seek to reach out to those outside your home? Can you be involved in ministry while maintaining a peaceful, loving home environment?

- Do you respect your husband when speaking with him or about him with others? Do you acknowledge God's plan for your husband's role in your home, a loving authority given by God to protect you and your family?

Peter also states, "Wives, in the same way be submissive to your husbands so that, if any of them do not believe the word, they may be won over without words by the behavior of their wives, when they see the purity and reverence of your lives" (1 Pet. 3:1–2).

Lorine Shannon, past coordinator of women's ministries for Grace Community Church in Sun Valley, California, writes in her manual *Lord, What Do You Want Me to Do?* "The woman who is the delight of her husband and her children, who has the imperishable quality of a gentle and quiet spirit, who has a hospitable attitude and charm, owes nothing to chance *because her outlook and influence has the solid foundation of the principle and wisdom of the Lord. . . . She is a vessel of honor.*"[1]

Identifying Your God-given Talents, Skills, or Abilities

Now that you have considered God's desires for women, the next step is to identify your specific gifts and abilities for service.

- Read Proverbs 31:10–30, and choose those qualities and skills you believe God is developing in your life. Make a list of these qualities and skills.

- Identify the advice others seek from you. Does it involve child care, personal relationships, or coping with emotions such as depression and anger, household management, interior decorating, wardrobe consultation, missionary concern, or other concerns?

- What do you enjoy most? Make a list of the things even when you cannot see how God might use them in a ministry. Pray that God will give you clear direction as you read further in this book.

- Describe one difficult experience in your life. How did God meet you at your point of deepest need?

Gigi Tchividjian, daughter of Billy and Ruth Graham, writes in her book *Diapers and Dishes or Pinstripes and Pumps*, "The Scriptures teach that at the moment of salvation, when we become a member of the body of Christ, which is the church, each of us is given a gift or gifts (see 1 Cor. 12). These gifts are uniquely suited for us and our particular situation or task."[2] You, too, have been given gifts. One joy in the Christian life is discovering these so that you can minister to others.

Joyce Turner, previous national women's coordinator for the Navigators, writes, "Each of us has at least one spiritual gift. Let us start where we are, use what we have and do what we can. Who knows what great things God has in mind, even with us!"[3]

As we seek to be Christ's body in the world, he equips us to fulfill our role in accomplishing his purposes. Cole Huffman, in his article "Meet Your Cell Mates," compares each member of Christ's body to a cell in the human body. Each is needed for the body to function to fulfill God's plan. "Life in the body of Christ is sustained by the interdependent function of individual believers. As 'cells,' believers serve the body as they relate to one another. Just like a cell, each believer carries out specialized work he or she was designed to do."[4]

As you continue in your walk with the Lord, ask the Lord for wisdom as you search for your particular gifts. In doing so, you will begin to recognize your friends', neighbors', and family's needs. Ask yourself, "Are there ways I can meet these needs?"

Ways to Recognize the Needs of Others and Minister to Them

- Have you ever considered jotting down problems and concerns expressed by friends and family in the course of a week? To do this, carry a small notebook with you to note remarks by others that allude to an unspoken need. You will be amazed at how this exercise enhances your sensitivity.

For example, you may write that a friend says, "It has been so hard caring for the children lately. Jim, my husband, has been working overtime for months. I feel like I never see him. Managing three children sure hasn't been easy."

When your friend mentions her difficulty in caring for her children, her words may be communicating a deeper message, one of loneliness or a feeling of neglect by her husband due to his job situation. How could God use you to comfort and encourage her?

- One excellent way to identify concerns, particularly if it involves a group of women, is through a survey. Choose and adapt the following surveys to obtain the exact information you are seeking. These can be used in a small group or local church setting to understand better the women in your sphere of influence.

Name: _____

Address: _____ Phone No.: _____

1. Please circle your age:

18–25 25–30 30–40 40–50 50–60 over 60

2. Please circle your marital status.

Single Married Divorced Widowed

3. Please write one pressing need you have in your life today.

4. Is another Christian or your church helping to meet this need?

The following questionnaire, developed by Mrs. Onilla May of Colorado Springs, Colorado, is circulated annually through every gathering at her church, including women's Bible studies and programs, Sunday school classes, choir, and new member classes. When the forms are completed and collected, a resource committee transfers all the information to specially printed three-by-five-inch cards which are filed by category. An alphabetical file and interests file enable the church to identify the interests of each woman and also help each of the women to use her gifts and talents in meeting needs within the church.

Women's Interest Survey

Name _____

Address _____

Phone _____ Place of employment _____

Work phone _____ Birthday _____

Member of this church ___ yes ___ no

Single __ Married __ Children _____ (list ages)

Every Christian needs a place of service where she is comfortable and where her interests and talents lie. We want to be sure that you are asked to serve in those areas where you have maximum effectiveness. Please write *interest* for those areas where you have a skill, talent, or an interest in serving. Write *experience* for those areas where you have had some previous experience—not necessarily in church situations.

Please feel free to write all over this paper! Please comment when it helps to clarify.

1. poster-making
   creating bulletin board
   design
   calligraphy
   printing name tags
   artistic design crafts (please list)
   crafts (please list)
   creative sewing
   painting or drawing
   floral arranging
   table decorating
   coordinating decorations
2. typing—typewriter/computer
   available _____
   bookkeeping office machines
   computers—type of experience ____
   preparing mailings
3. working with ideas
   creating program themes
   planning women's ministry projects
4. writing letters
   writing job descriptions
   writing announcements,
       publicity, press releases
   journalism experience

5. writing skits

   writing plays

   acting in skits or plays

   directing dramatic presentations

   designing stage sets for

      dramatic productions

   painting scenery for stage

      sets

6. baking, cooking

   sewing, using patterns

   driving—vehicle available ___

   indoor or outdoor gardening

   helping behind the scenes

   like to work alone

   like to shop, collect

      materials for projects or

      programs

   I own a collection of _____

   interest in reading—have extensive library

7. will open my home for meetings on

      occasion

   will accommodate overnight guests of the

      church on occasion

   will help to serve meals at the church on

      occasion

   wedding receptions or other hosting at

      church

8. managing people

   organizing people, programs

small-group leader

large-group leader

9. conducting musical

   groups

vocal soloist

choir participant

other groups

music experience ___

instruments played ___

operating sound equipment ___

experience ___

sound equipment owned ___

10. working with people

motivating people

greeter

public speaking

telephoning

social director

friendship visitation in homes

hospital visitation

will give personal testimony

evangelism training

   completed here ___

   another church ___

prayer ministry good with children

counseling

11. photography—camera

available _____

developing at home

projectionist

portrait photographer

experience or training in photography ___

12. athletic interest ___

coaching experience ___

sport(s) ___

aerobics instructor

other physical fitness

involvement:

13. Christian education committee, training

teaching:

nursery

toddlers

preschool

grades 1–3

grades 4–6

grades 7–9

grades 10–12

college-level groups women

assisting in the above ____

14. other areas I am interested in

15. educational background _____

16. religious background or training ___

17. my spiritual gift

Take time to fill in this survey. You may be surprised at your many God-given skills and abilities that can be used by him to minister to others. After each person fills in the above Women's Interest Survey, the results can be placed in a categorized file system so that specific women can be identified who possess the gifts needed for recognized areas.

Categorized File System

People Oriented _____
(Name)   (Telephone)

_____ working with, motivating   _____ hospital visitation

_____ greeter   _____ testimony

_____ public speaking experience   _____ evangelism training

_____ telephoning   _____ child care

_____ social director   _____ counseling

_____ friendship & visitation   _____ teacher, speaker

Photographer _____
(Name)   (Telephone)

_____ camera available   _____ projectionist

_____ developing experience   _____ portrait photographer

Clerical _____
(Name)   (Telephone)

_____ typing   _____ office machines

_____ filing   _____ computers

_____ bookkeeping   _____ mailings

Creative Thinker _____
(Name)   (Telephone)

_____ ideas   _____ projects

_____ programs   _____ themes

Creative Writer _____

                       (Name)   (Telephone)

_____ writing letters

_____ writing job descriptions

_____ writing announcements, publicity, press releases

_____ journalism experience

Drama _____

                       (Name)   (Telephone)

_____ writing skits   _____ directing

_____ writing plays   _____ designing

_____ acting   _____ painting sets

Helper/Server _____

                       (Name)   (Telephone)

_____ baking

_____ sewing

_____ driving—vehicle available _____

_____ gardening

_____ helping behind the scenes

_____ like to work alone

_____ like to shop, collect materials _____

_____ owns collection of _____

_____ reading

Hospitality _____

                     (Name)   (Telephone)

_____ will open home for meetings

_____ will accommodate overnight guests

_____ will help serve meals

_____ wedding receptions or other hostess duties at church

Leader _____
                              (Name)   (Telephone)

_____ managing people

_____ organizing people, programs

_____ small-group leader

_____ large-group leader

Music/Sound _____
                              (Name)   (Telephone)

_____ conducting

_____ vocalist-accompanies self _____ uses tapes _____

_____ choir

_____ other group _____

instruments played _____

sound experience _____

instruments owned _____

experience _____ equipment owned _____

training _____

Physical fitness _____
                              (Name)   (Telephone)

_____ athletics

_____ coaching—experience

_____ aerobics instructor

_____ other _____

Teacher/Spiritual Leader _____
                              (Name)   (Telephone)

_____ Christian education committee

_____ teaching experience

_____ assisting

_____ religious background

spiritual gift _____

teaching style _____

personality profile _____

Artistic _____

                (Name)   (Telephone)

_____ poster-making   _____ floral arranging

_____ bulletin board   _____ table decorating

_____ calligraphy   _____ decorations coordinator

_____ printing name tags   _____ design

_____ painting—medium _____   _____ sewing

Alphabetical File System

Date _____

Name _____ Member _____

Address _____ S.M.Ch _____

Phone _____ Employed _____

Ph _____ Birthday _____

Interests

___ Artistic–1	___ Drama–5	___ Music/Sound–9
___ Clerical–2	___ Helper/Server–6	___ People Oriented–10
___ Creative Thinker–3	___ Hospitality–7	___ Photography–11
___ Creative Writer–4	___ Leader–8	___ Physical–12
		___ Teacher–13

Now that you have considered your biblical role as a woman, discovered your personal talents, gifts, and abilities, and learned ways to identify the needs of others for ministry opportunities, it is time to search for God's unique purpose for you. In the following pages you will find a variety of creative and alternative views for Christian women's ministry. Remember to pray that you will be sensitive to the Holy Spirit's prompting as he directs you into a specific ministry.

We will return to the Personal Inventory Questionnaire in the final chapter and evaluate your answers based on the ministry opportunities you will read about in the *Resource Guide for Women's Ministry.*

"For God . . . made his light shine in our hearts to give us the light of the knowledge of the glory of God in the face of Christ. But we have this treasure in jars of clay to show that this all-surpassing power is from God and not from us" (2 Cor. 4:6–7).

Chapter 2

WOMEN LEADING PRAYER EFFECTIVELY

It couldn't have been a more beautiful spring day. Brilliant pink and red azaleas dotted the green landscape surrounding the church. The sun's heat tanned my face. I waited at the foot of the steps for the newlyweds to burst through the huge oak church doors. Chattering, excited voices drifted over me.

As I scanned the crowd, one woman in particular held my attention. She was the mother of the bride and in animated conversation with the pastor. Soon she finished her conversation and moved down the steps toward me.

"Linda, I do hope that we can get together soon. I'd love to tell you my story. As I mentioned, I'm living proof God can use anyone who loves Jesus Christ, even an everyday housewife like me," she said as she flashed me a grin. I had immediately liked this dark-haired, brown-eyed woman with her gracious smile and rich Southern drawl. I assured her I would look forward to hearing her story.

Months later on a hot August afternoon, I had the privilege of meeting with Mary Lance Sisk. Later I discovered that she was the prayer chairman for Leighton Ford Ministries and a board member for the Joni and Friends organization. Her teachings on prayer were published monthly in Joni's newsletter. For several years Mary Lance led a weekly prayer group and teaching session in her local church. At one time she was an administrative leader for Lydia Fellowship.

In the captivating interview that followed our meeting, Mary Lance talked about the imperative need for prayer prior to beginning any ministry. She introduced ways to enhance your prayer life and offered practical ideas for forming and leading prayer groups. Prayer is the first step in identifying God's will for his ministry in and through your life. Mary Lance's insights prepare you to listen to God and hear his voice through prayer. It enables you to begin or enhance a vibrant life of personal prayer.

LRM: Mary Lance, how did the Lord lead you into this focus on prayer? How did you get started?

MLS: It started in January 1975, six weeks after my conversion. God reached me on my blind side. I was invited to lunch by two good Christian friends, Sara and Lillian. After lunch they suggested that we have a time of prayer.

Linda, I panicked. I had never prayed aloud in front of

anybody, unless it was the Lord's Prayer with a group of people. I had always read prayers out of a prayer book.

Lillian prayed first, and it was in magnificent King James English. Sara followed with an eloquent prayer in American English. Both prayed extraordinary and beautiful prayers, and then it was my turn.

I was so scared I didn't know what to do. My heart was pounding as they were praying and I was wondering what I was going to say.

I honestly heard the voice of the Lord speak to my heart. God told me to pray the truth.

LRM: What exactly did you pray?

MLS: Lord Jesus Christ, You know I don't know how to pray. Lord, teach me to pray. I didn't know that I was praying the Word of God. The Lord answered my prayer. God had me pray his Word, found in Luke 11:1. Still studying in Matthew, I didn't have a clue that the prayer was in the Bible, but God did.

LRM: How did God answer that prayer?

MLS: During the next four years, I didn't realize it, but he was teaching me God's way to pray. He was doing it. I had no clue what was going on.

LRM: How did he do this? Through personal Bible study, conferences?

MLS: He taught me through the Word of God. God can teach you through his Word. From 1975 to 1980, I learned about prayer by being alone with the Holy Spirit. The most significant thing God taught me during that time was forgiveness, the key to mountain-moving prayer.

We are called by God to love everybody in the world without reserve, and we must do it. I don't think you can have a decent prayer life without forgiveness.

LRM: Tell me more about your time alone with God.

MLS: The Word of God says in John 15:7, "If you abide in me, and my words abide in you, ask whatever you will, and it shall be done for you" (RSV). I find that if I sit before the Lord, he gives me the Scripture verses to pray for others.

I start my quiet time with great humility, with thanksgiving and praise. I then have my regular morning reading. When I read the Word, certain verses jump out at me. That's God voice. God shows me what to include in my prayers from my reading of the Scriptures.

I pray those particular verses for my family, for leaders in the nations, for the government, and so forth.

LRM: In other words, as you come before the Lord, you say, "Father, as I read the Word today, would you show me the Scriptures you want me to pray during this day?"

MLS: Yes. The most important thing is not to rush it, not to rush having a prayer life. It will evolve. God tells us, "The one who calls you is faithful and he will do it" (1 Thess. 5:24). If you want a prayer life, he will give you one. You don't need to be worried about it.

I find so many women greatly frustrated because they aren't praying like this. It takes time to develop a prayer life. Many years ago I prayed that first prayer, "Lord Jesus, teach me to pray." God's worked hard in those years. I don't feel like I'm even close to being where I want to be, but I know it takes time, and I know he's faithful.

LRM: If you knew someone who wanted to begin reaching out to other women in prayer so that their prayer life might grow, how would you counsel her? What should she do?

MLS: First, everyone needs time with God. That's the beginning. In my opinion, it helps to begin alone and then pray with a partner.

LRM: When the Lord brings forth that prayer partner, how do you structure your time together? Do you have a prayer strategy?

MLS: Yes. My partner and I set aside a regular time each week to pray together. My present prayer partner and I pray for the nations of the world. My first prayer partner and I prayed for personal needs. When women first start praying, they are overwhelmed by the enormity of the task.

For example, I believe that when God puts you in a specific neighborhood, he's called you to pray for that neighborhood. He doesn't call you to start praying for everybody in the neighborhood at one time.

In my neighborhood I specifically pray every day for the five homes around my house, instead of every house on the street. God might call somebody to start praying for just one family on the street. The problem is that people try to take on too much at one time, and they quit.

LRM: Can you give us a brief example of the prayer strategy?

MLS: I think it's important to have goals and have a plan to reach those goals. Let me give you an example. God tells us in 1 Timothy 2:1–4 to pray for all those in authority. How in the world can you do that?

What I do is set daily goals and weekly goals. For example, in my daily goals, I pray for the president of the United States, the governor of my state, and the mayor of my city. In one week, I want to pray for all the leaders in the government whom God wants me to pray for, so I have a daily strategy to help me reach these weekly goals.

LRM: What about the young mother whose time is limited and who sincerely wants to develop an effective prayer life and even begin a prayer ministry with other women?

MLS: She may not feel that she can give as much time alone as someone like me, and that's true. However, what she can do is make a choice to get up earlier in the morning and have time alone with God, spending an hour in the morning with God before her family wakes up.

This truly demonstrates Proverbs 31. The woman in Proverbs 31 awoke early to get food for her household, and I call that spiritual food. Another thing a young mother can do to have a good prayer life is to put up a map of a nation on the refrigerator. Every time she goes in the kitchen she can say a prayer for a different nation. She can put pictures of missionaries who are working in that nation on the refrigerator too. During the day she can use it for prayer each time she passes by.

Mirrors in bathrooms are other spots for pictures, typed Scripture verses, or other reminders. Keep a list of people in your car and pray for them as you drive. However, don't set goals you cannot reach. Start off slowly. Compared to today, the way I prayed four years ago is as different as night and day. God spent time teaching me to pray. He works it into our lives.

Mary Lance Sisk has given us foundational principles about prayer. Prayer must precede the planning of any program or the pursuit of any ministry. And Evelyn Christianson has gone a step further in saying, God expects us to be orderly. He expects us to discipline ourselves by managing our prayer time well in order to prepare well-planned programs.[1] If we could learn to pray first and plan afterward, our homes, churches, Christian women's clubs, and Bible studies—whatever we are doing for Christ—would be different. Maybe, just maybe, we are going in one direction and God's will is aimed at another. God might say, "Hold everything. This is not my will for you, not that way."

Beginning a Prayer Ministry

Let's assume you have established a personal prayer time in your daily life and have possibly joined with a prayer partner for weekly prayer sessions. Yet you feel as if God is calling you to something more. Maybe God is leading you to begin a prayer ministry in your home or church.

The first question to be answered is, What is the value of gathering others together for prayer? J. Oswald Sanders writes in his book *Prayer Power Unlimited*, "When a number of Christians unite in prayer for a given person or objective, it is the uniform teaching of Scripture that brings special spiritual power into operation, for their gathering demonstrates the oneness that God delights to see and acknowledge."[2]

We find many examples throughout the Bible where God's people unite for prayer. In Exodus, God told Moses to call the people together to meet with him at Mount Sinai. In Acts 4:23–31, we see New Testament Christians united to speak with God. In each case God mightily answers their prayers, showing his person and pleasure.

In her book *Prayer: Conversing with God,* Rosalind Rinker lists several reasons Christians should pray together. First, "because Jesus promised that when two of his disciples (that means us today) meet to pray, he will be there with them (Matt. 18:20). In a particular way, in a particular promise, he is there."

The second reason she suggests is that we will find shared burdens become lighter. Paul tells us to "bear one another's burdens" (Gal. 6:2 RSV).

Rinker's third reason is, "As we pray the Spirit of our Lord has our attention. . . . He can whisper to us the love plans he has for us. Sometimes these directions come to two or more persons in the group at the same time. We find ourselves in total agreement."

Her fourth point is that "when we pray together we become bold and honest" with God.

And finally, "The more we pray with other people . . . self-consciousness drops away and we can pray about our real problems, not just surface ones. Genuine 'togetherness' is a God-given state, and hearts are joined in His presence."[3]

When Jesus was asked by a man how to pray, the only complete prayer Jesus provided begins with *Our* Father (Matt. 6:9). He intends for us to pray together "one in heart and mind" (Acts 4:32).

Organizing a Prayer Group

Where do you begin? With prayer, of course. Pray that God will reveal to you those individuals with whom you should pray. Contact each one personally. Allow them time to pray about their involvement and then arrange to meet in a home for the first time.

Of the three hundred women surveyed at a recent women's conference, 99.5 percent said small-group prayer sessions made up of three to twelve women were the most successful. If the first meeting is to be held in the church, insert a notice in the Sunday bulletin. Invite all women who are interested in meeting weekly for prayer.

If many women respond after an initial opening time of introduction, break into small groups of six or eight and meet in separate rooms in the building. Plan a time for corporate prayer at a central location to close the meeting.

As a leader, you provide the prayer group's course. Group leaders do not dominate or control. It is their responsibility to be sensitive to the Holy Spirit's guidance and direction.

As Mary Lance Sisk mentioned, she and one of her prayer partners prayed about personal needs and concerns. With another partner, prayer for the nations was the focus. Ask God for his purposes and direction in forming your particular group or groups. Direct prayer according to this purpose.

"[Without] vision, the people perish" (Prov. 29:18 KJV). Without direction, a prayer group can quickly dissolve into a social occasion or one in which problems are discussed. Prayer may be placed on the back burner. Two essential elements to every prayer group are direction and confidentiality.

Listed below are some of the creative ways you can direct women in prayer. Many of these have been proven effective in the prayer ministry of Mabel Dumas of Greenville, Texas.

1. Ask each woman to write prayer requests when she arrives. Put these slips of paper in a box. Have each woman choose a request and lead the others in prayer concerning that specific need.

2. Before prayer time at each meeting, have one of the participants present a brief devotional on different aspects of prayer. Use the cited Scriptures in the devotional to give prayer direction.

3. Before the women arrive, make a list of specific physical, spiritual, and emotional needs of individuals in the group. The list may be distributed to the participants. Individuals may remain anonymous.

4. At one of the meetings, focus on missions and missionaries. Bring letters from missionaries to read and indicate specific needs. Identify the mission field on a map of the world and give information about the country and people to help everyone identify with the missionaries' work there.

5. On another day pray for husbands and children, enabling each woman to express heartfelt concerns or claim a Scripture verse for each family member.

6. Pray for the leaders of different countries around the world or for a specific situation in a particular country.

7. Pray for Christians around the world, particularly those who are harassed or persecuted.

8. At Christmastime, have a prayer birthday party for Jesus. Each person brings an inspirational quote or Scripture verse wrapped in a decorated box to be opened and read after the prayer time.

9. Also at Christmas, respond to Romans 12:1–2 by having each woman kneel at an altar (coffee table) and say what she plans to give Jesus this year.

10. Distribute small papers with a specific name of God and its meaning printed on it. Through group prayer, help each woman see that God is the "I am" for every situation in her life.

11. Have each woman claim one of God's promises that applies to a difficult situation she is facing and pray accordingly.

12. Pray for the church leaders.

13. Lead an entire prayer time in song, with each woman praying the words of favorite hymns and choruses as they are sung by the group. Choose hymns or choruses that focus on one topic such as thanksgiving, praise, or characteristics of God.

14. Collect articles from the local newspaper and pray for the specific needs in your community.

15. Ask an international student to come and talk about or show slides of his or her country. Pray afterward for the country.

16. Slowly read a Scripture passage in Psalms or Proverbs, leaving a brief period of silence for prayers after each verse.

17. Write a brief prayer concerning the familiar topics of adoration, confession, thanksgiving, and supplication. Ask different women to read each prayer. Follow with spontaneous prayer and silence before reading the next prayer.

18. Read a chapter a week from a book on prayer. Discuss and apply the principles mentioned.

19. Conduct an inductive Bible study throughout the week and ask each woman to bring to the prayer time a sentence that describes a personal application she would like to pray about in her own life.

20. Establish yearly goals for prayer.

21. Say sentence prayers as topics are mentioned.

22. Spend an entire meeting in prayer to God, thanking him for answered prayer which builds faith and trust in him.

23. Send theme-related Scripture verses to small-group members to focus minds and hearts on the meeting.

24. Set aside one meeting to pray for school students by name. After the prayer meeting, care packages of food and inexpensive gifts could be prepared and mailed to out-of-town college students.

25. Begin the prayer time by setting aside ten minutes to read a chapter from a book of the Bible. The books of the Bible would be covered gradually by year's end. Spend five minutes in quiet meditation; then have a few volunteers read a meaningful verse aloud. Spontaneous prayers could follow for the remainder of the time.

26. Write prayer requests on cards and distribute. After corporate prayer and praise, each woman takes a card, finds a quiet place, and prays alone for those prayer requests listed on the card.

27. Distribute blank cards and have each woman write a "mountain" problem if there is one and leave the card unsigned. Pass the cards around the small group and ask each woman to pray aloud for the need expressed on the card.

28. Go around the small-group circle, giving each woman five minutes to tell of one need in her life and one praise to her heavenly Father. One member of the group then prays for that woman before moving on to another.

29. End prayer time with a period of silence, asking the Holy Spirit to bring to mind any overlooked areas of prayers or subjects not mentioned. Close this prayer time with the women standing in a circle, holding one another's hands, and praying out of love for the woman on her right.

30. Prior to the meeting, send a letter explaining that at a special time there will be no more conversation. All are free to chat as members arrive, but at a specific time all will be quiet. Prayer will begin approximately ten minutes later and continue until the end of the meeting. Everyone leaves in silence.

These are just a few of the many creative ways you can lead women in fresh, meaningful prayer sessions. Emily Prince of Clinton, Mississippi, writes, "Three friends and I were led by God to meet weekly for prayer. We have coffee and each takes a turn to share her deepest, most heartfelt praises and petitions.

"Then we go to the throne of grace in prayer. We usually go around the circle and each prays for one other woman in the group. We spend two and one-half hours together on a weeknight. This special time ministers to our souls, offering encouragement and support. Many of our prayers have been marvelously answered, and we have grown in our daily walk with Christ."

Opportunities for prayer are unlimited. Have you considered beginning a day of prayer, organizing a telephone prayer chain, or celebrating a holiday with prayer?

Planning a Prayer Retreat

Onilla May of Colorado Springs, Colorado, described a day of prayer retreat that she began in the church she attends. A morning was set aside for prayer at the church. Her theme for the retreat was taken from Revelation 5:8: "The four living creatures and the twenty-four elders fell down before the Lamb. . . . They were holding golden bowls full of incense, which are the prayers of the saints."

In keeping with the theme, large brass vases were placed around the sanctuary to represent gold bowls. Potpourri simmered throughout the room, symbolizing the mentioned fragrance. The format of prayer related to adoration, confession, thanksgiving, and supplication. The women directing each prayer read segments aloud that related to aspects of the listed prayer, leaving pauses after each word or phrase for silent prayer. The program was as follows:

Day of Prayer

Welcome
The Ministry of Prayer
"The Lord's Prayer"
Songs of Praise

Prayer

Adoration
    Pray a brief, one- or two-sentence prayer of praise to God.

Those who pray aloud, please stand to be heard; others remain seated.

Confession

Pray silently, asking God to search the darkest corners of our hearts, showing us our own sin. Confess any:

Words—Slander, gossip, corruption, criticism, lies, obscenities, spite, lacking love.

Attitudes—Anger, hatred, bitterness, lack of love, pride, rebellion, jealousy, envy, selfishness, malice, conceit, unforgiving, greed, spirit of independence from God.

Actions—Self-seeking, failing to forgive, failing to ask forgiveness, stealing, sloth, gluttony, boasting, deception, pleasure seeking, idolatry, unfaithfulness, sexual immorality, adultery, failing to do the good we know to do, prayerlessness.

Thoughts—Impure, sensuous, lustful.

Thanksgiving

Pray a corporate prayer, agreeing with those who lead. Women throughout the congregation rise and spontaneously pray.

Supplication

(Please stand.) Pray in a directed prayer. Please lead in prayer aloud as you are led by the Holy Spirit. Please pray for:

The World—All people groups to be reached with the gospel of the Lord Jesus Christ.

Our Nation—Our people to put away the sins of our nation and culture. God to bring into government people of faith and character.

Our State—God to raise up Christian leaders.

Our City—Christians throughout our city to be the light of Christ in their world. Our mayor and city council to turn to the Lord for wisdom and direction. (Please be seated.)

Musical Interlude

Sing a worshipful duet.

Supplication

Individuals stand and lead in prayer for the following requests and other requests as they come to mind through the Holy Spirit's leading.

Our Homes—Love and respect of family members for one another. Guard against evil influences of television. The needs of working mothers and single parents. Exalt the Word of God.

Our Children—A heart for God, a hunger for his Word, and protection from contamination of worldly lifestyles.

Our Church—Hearts of the people turned to God. People to pursue spiritual growth through knowledge of the Word and prayer. People to share the gospel and disciple new believers. Our people to learn to give biblically. Vision for the mission and future of churches. The leaders and entire staff to receive God's power and energy for perseverance, to encourage one another and experience a bond of unity in a spirit of peace.

Musical Interlude

Sing a praise chorus.

Supplication

Pray for each leader by name, including Sunday school teachers. Each ministry as a whole is prayed for.

Musical Interlude

Worshipful solo is sung.

Supplication

Pray for the women in the church.

The Leadership—Complete dependence on God, ability to make wise decisions, genuine love and caring for one another, unity of purpose, vision for the ministry, protection in spiritual welfare, multiplied time and energy, good health.

The Ministries—Women's Bible studies. Women to attend who have never attended before, women hungry to know the Word and eager for spiritual growth, encouragement for the teachers, the Holy Spirit's leading to be evident in each group, women willing to disciple others and show them the way to greater obedience to Christ.

Sisters in serving. Women to have a heart of compassion and consolation for the sick; the ability lovingly to involve others in the congregation in ministries such as greeting, hospitality, and friendship; a heart for the ministry of prayer; and a commitment to intercede for others faithfully.

Fellowship ministries. Women experiencing biblical fellowship, encouraging one another, loving and supporting one another as they participate in other church ministries.

Missions. The urgency of taking the gospel to all nations to become a reality to women in our church. A conviction to pray for and support the work of our missionaries.

Musical Interlude

Sing Alleluia to the Lord.

Personal Prayer Needs

Individual prayer requests are taken from the cards and corporate prayer is given. (Please stand.)

Closing Hymn

At another church, one prayer segment on the actual agenda was led by a woman who called for a time of silent adoration by reading Psalm 103 and pausing between verses. Then areas of sin were named with pauses for silent confession.

During a period of thanksgiving following the reading, all women stood and together thanked God for answering personal prayers. Finally, each took the hand of one or two women and prayed aloud the personal supplications of their hearts.

During the interview mentioned earlier, Mary Lance Sisk addressed the planning of all-day prayer retreats.

LRM: How do you structure a prayer retreat?

MLS: First, I ask God what he wants for each prayer retreat. I believe the Lord gives me a theme from his Word. Then I use the following format for the retreat.

9:30–10:00 a.m.	Praise and worship time
10:00–10:30 a.m.	Presentation of theme and Scriptures

10:30–11:00 a.m.	Private prayer and meditation
11:00–11:15 a.m.	Break
11:15–12:15 p.m.	Small-group meeting to share what is learned from God during meditation and group prayer times.
12:15–1:15 p.m.	Lunch
1:15–1:45 p.m.	Come together for reports by each small group.
1:45–3:30 p.m.	The remaining time is spent in corporate prayer with: (1) individual prayers expressed first, (2) directed prayers (selected topics), leaving pauses for silent prayers to follow.

Try to incorporate three types of prayer: prayer alone with God, prayer in small groups, and corporate prayer. During corporate prayer, women may pray individually in the large group and simultaneously at other times.

One format that emphasizes variety includes hymn singing, group prayer, hymn singing, prayer in pairs, hymn singing, individual prayers, and closing with group prayer. Another group incorporated fasting in their prayer retreat. Only water was allowed.

Organizing a Prayer Chain

Telephone prayer chains can also be an instrument for uniting women for prayer sessions. This is strictly voluntary; no one is pressured to participate. All who are interested in praying are grouped under a number of leaders. The group leader's name appears at the beginning and end of each list so she can be certain that each member of the chain is contacted. The names and telephone numbers of each member are listed.

Any person can call the prayer-chain coordinator, day or night, and be assured that each person will be contacted for prayer. When the coordinator receives a prayer request, she calls the first woman on her list, and the chain is activated. Each person is responsible for calling the person whose name is next on the list, after she is called. This is one way in which private prayer can become a corporate endeavor.

Another program is used at Ridgecrest Baptist Church, Greenville, Texas, and is entitled Operation Glory. One weekend each month church members sign up for a thirty-minute time segment totaling a twenty-four-hour day (Saturday morning to Sunday morning). Prayer guides are written for use by participants. It is possible for three or four people to be praying at the same time about the same subject. This is an attempt to have people pray as a body of believers. The following guide is an example of one way to use a program like this.

A Time to Praise

"Blessed be the LORD my strength" (Ps. 144:1 KJV).

"Every day I will bless thee. . . . Great is the LORD, and greatly to be praised" (Ps. 145:2–3 KJV).

"Praise is the soul in flower. Praising God is one of the highest and purest acts of religion. In prayer we act like Men; in Praise we act like angels."

—Thomas Watson

"Self-love may lead us to prayers, but love to God excites us to praises."

—Thomas Manton

"Alas, for that capital crime of the Lord's people . . . barrenness in Praises! Oh, how fully I am persuaded that an hour of praise is worth a day of fasting and mourning."

—John Livingston

Now, let us enter into an experience of praise:

Sing: "Every day is a glory day. Every day is a glory day. Every day is a glory day. When you put it into the hands of the Lord."

Now do it! Don't just sing about doing it. Do it! Ask the Lord to take your day and do with it and you whatever pleases him. Don't be surprised at what happens to you today! Now let's walk through some steps of praise.

Step 1. Tell God that you love him because of *who* he is. Then list at least six titles that flood your heart. For example, say, "I love you because you are my Father, my Savior, my Protector, my Pace Setter, and my El Shaddai." Please attempt to make a different list—your own names for God.

Step 2. Sing God a praise song.

1. Make one of your own. Go ahead, even if you've never tried.

2. Read one from a hymnal, but select one that you can change into personal pronouns. Now you are singing a personal praise song to him, not just repeating the words of a praise song to him.

3. Or you may select a simple chorus used from memory. Now speak a word of praise to someone. Determine what and who you will speak to.

• Tell boldly about an answer to prayer that you have experienced.

• Write your intention. Tell in some detail just how good God is and how good it is to know him on a daily basis. Choose your words carefully.

• Try to put into words his peace that permeates your life or something else equally hard. This is not easy. Don't expect it to be. Now you are ready to pray.

Be specific as you pray. Write down your request. Praise him for the answers. Keep them and record when and how he answers your requests.

Other prayer guides could include selected portions of a book about prayer, teaching on hindrances to prayer, or a list of identified sins needing confession before prayer. Quotes, Scripture verses, and poems can be used as well as specific prayer requests.

Many small and large groups of women have original approaches to prayer that have value for others.

Jane Holbrook of Fort Lauderdale, Florida, described one special prayer program. "I belong to a small prayer group that meets once a month. The hostess serves lunch, and then we spend an hour or two in prayer for a missionary or missionaries. To sponsor a missionary, each woman pays $15 to attend this luncheon, and the collected money is sent to the missionary of the month."

In Volant, Pennsylvania, Marg Maguire described a college prayer meeting she vividly remembers. "I was part of an all-night prayer meeting on New Year's Eve. We wanted to bring in the new year with the Lord. We introduced a topic and prayed for fifteen to twenty minutes about it. We'd break for refreshments and then continue."

Dean Black of Jackson, Mississippi, tells of a memorable prayer group in her life. "A group of people from our church who had experienced recent deaths in their families met biweekly for prayer and testimonials. This helped us all through our grief."

The possibilities are limitless. Ask God to show you his plan as you desire to grow in your own prayer life and lead others in united prayer. Ray Stedman writes in his book *Talking to My Father,* "The power of the Church does not rest in its numbers, its status, its wealth, its money, its position. The power of the Church of Jesus Christ rests in its prayers."[4]

Chapter 3

ONE-ON-ONE AND SMALL-
GROUP DISCIPLESHIP

Dear Linda,

Thank you for your note. The Lord has used different people at different times to encourage me, and you are part of that. It was so good to hear from you and get such a good report.

Much love, Elzanne

ELZANNE, A YOUNG WOMAN, died a few months later. The fatal disease took her life but couldn't defeat her faith. She was small in stature with shoulder-length hair. Her withered hands and tightly drawn mouth were caused by the debilitating disease. Yet Elzanne had a love for God and an indomitable will to please him that could not be stopped.

My first encounter with Elzanne followed a church gathering. Naturally shy, she asked if she could speak with me alone.

I readily agreed, and we made an appointment. I had no idea what was on her mind.

The following week, when I was sitting across from her at a child's Sunday school table, she said that she felt a deep need to grow spiritually. I realized she was also looking for a friend. She asked if I would be willing to meet with her once a week.

I felt awkward because of my inexperience with one-on-one discipleship. I wasn't sure about the long-term commitment that would be involved, but I accepted her invitation. That was to become one of the most meaningful relationships I had during my stay in Texas.

The next Thursday we met in Elzanne's home. First, we shared our personal experiences of meeting Christ. Then we decided that each week we'd consider and discuss a Bible verse that had meant a lot to us in our daily quiet time that week.

Over the next two years our friendship grew. We continually challenged and encouraged each other. Laughter, joy, tears, and disappointments bound us together. Elzanne's commitment to obediently act out her living faith challenged me.

After her death others discovered that Elzanne had touched many lives with a kind note, caring visit, small gifts of food, or an invitation to come with her to church. As I reflected on Elzanne's witness, I remembered a time when our family was planning a vacation.

The afternoon before we left, Elzanne prepared a special bag of goodies, games, and coloring activities for each of my children. This was just one example of the caring she showed. A woman who knew pain, disease, and inevitable death, she yearned to express her love for God and consistently thought of others.

We live in a transient society. Many of us hesitate to establish deep relationships with others. We may become isolated and aloof because we fear future separations or because of the habit of withholding ourselves. We are threatened by our vulnerability and fear that others will come to know us as we really are.

Yet we find peace in Jesus' final prayer as he prepared to leave his disciples, "Holy Father, protect them by the power of your name—the name you gave me—so that they may be one as we are one" (John 17:11).

It is not only God's will that we participate in, support, and encourage other believers; doing so is also a teaching tool. We learn how to be Christ's disciples, reflecting his nature and character as we see his work and person reflected in other believers.

The dictionary defines *disciple* as a learner, a pupil, or a follower of Jesus Christ. It is also defined as one who accepts and assists in spreading the doctrines of another in his lifetime. We, the followers of Jesus Christ, are called by God to learn from and teach others how to become disciples who clearly reflect Christ.

Written in Scriptures for women in particular we read, "Teach the older women to be reverent in the way they live, not to be slanderers or addicted to much wine, but to teach what is good. Then they can train the younger women to love their husbands and children, to be self-controlled and pure, to be busy at home, to be kind, and to be subject to their husbands, so that no one will malign the word of God" (Titus 2:3–5).

Whether you take these verses to represent chronological age or spiritual maturity, you as a believer are being observed as an example of the Christian's way of life. Whether the observer is a child, a young neighbor, an elderly widow, or your mother-in-law, you are discipling someone or teaching someone in the ways of the Christian life.

Susan Hunt, in her article "Reach Out and Comfort Someone," says to older women: "Your 'longevity' does not make you out-dated; it makes you credible. Please teach us (younger women) what you have learned of the faithfulness of our Heavenly Father and share with us practical ways we can comfort women who experience what you have experienced."[1]

A young woman who knows and has experienced the Lord can disciple other young women. Paul writes to Timothy, "Let no man despise thy youth" (1 Tim. 4:12 KJV).

In his article "The Value of a Caring Community," Ralph Wilson writes, "Christian fellowship is essential to our spiritual health." He gives four reasons for this:

1. To maintain Christian values we need to be part of a distinctly Christian community so that we and our children are better able to resist the pressures of the secular world. "We share our struggles, we stand against the tide; we teach the faith."

2. To keep us spiritually healthy, God gives various members of the body specific tools, specific gifts to help us carry on his work. There may be someone ready to help who is especially equipped by God to do so.

3. God uses believers as role models. We can see the fruit of the Spirit in certain people who clearly show Christ's character. This serves as an example and impetus for us to stretch and grow.

4. When people watch out for one another with love in the

church, it is Christian fellowship at its best. "Carry each others' burdens, and in this way . . . fulfill the law of Christ" (Gal. 6:2).[2]

How can you be obedient to God in this area of discipleship? Is God calling you to meet alone with a Christian friend, peer, or teenager who is struggling with some area of faith? Does someone need you to go alongside them during a time of crisis?

Our first act of discipleship should be the constant desire to be "conformed to the likeness of his Son" (Rom. 8:29). We should desire to be like our Master. Matthew wrote, "A student is not above his teacher, nor a servant above his master. It is enough for the student to *be* like his teacher, and the servant like his master" (Matt. 10:24–25).

We become like our Master by reading God's Word and listening to his voice. Isaiah wrote: "The Sovereign LORD has given me an instructed tongue, to know the word that sustains the weary. He awakens me morning by morning, wakens my ear to listen like one being taught" (50:4).

Second, Jesus describes the qualifications for a disciple. Again in Matthew, we find, "Therefore every teacher of the law who has been instructed about the kingdom of heaven is like the owner of a house who brings out of his storeroom new treasures as well as old" (13:52).

As disciples we: (1) need to be walking with Jesus Christ, (2) are accountable for learning new truths from his Word as well as reflecting on old truths, and (3) communicate these truths as well as God's faithfulness in our life experiences.

This is our commission. In a ministry newsletter from Vienna, Austria, written prior to the fall of the Iron Curtain, Myrna Alexander tells of a woman who understood the need for each disciple to communicate the truths she learned. The newsletter read, "The face and words of an earnest young mother with leg braces is a particular charge."

Myrna marveled at the determined concentration and the careful note-taking of this young woman who had slipped away unseen to attend this meeting of the underground church. The woman's response was, "We who have been privileged to hear the Bible taught now have the responsibility to share accurately these words with others."

With added emphasis the young woman continued, "Most of all I want my children to know the truths of Scripture which have been shared today. If I don't teach them, they will not hear! There are many other mothers who share my burden. But God has allowed me to be here because of my crippled state, and I have the time to take this teaching to mothers who, like myself, want their children to know God."

A third aspect of discipleship is self-sacrificing commitment. Jesus' words are uncompromising: "If anyone comes to me and does not hate his father and mother, his wife and children, his brothers and sisters—yes, even his own life—he cannot be my disciple. . . . In the same way, any of you who does not give up everything he has cannot be my disciple" (Luke 14:26–27, 33).

Does Jesus want us to hate our relatives and give up everything to become his disciple? No, he wants us to love him more than anyone or anything. He must hold first place in every area of our lives.

Barbara Barker of Birmingham, Alabama, speaker and pastor's wife, has said, "In the Christian life it really has to be 'not I, but Christ liveth in me. The life which I now live in the flesh (cooking, serving, being a mother, being a wife, being a friend) I live not by my strength in the security of my abilities and talents, but by the faith of the Son of God who loved me and gave himself for me.' He gave not just to pay for my sins but also to give me his life so that he might use me as an instrument to demonstrate who he is to the world that wants to know, 'Is He real?'"

When we live with a desire to be conformed to the image of Jesus Christ, placing him first in our lives, we are ready to encourage others in this pursuit. Today *mentoring* is another word used to describe discipleship. A *mentor* is defined as a wise, loyal advisor, a teacher, or a coach.

Dee Brestin, in her book *The Friendship of Women* says, "In discipling, you meet with someone regularly to learn how to study the Bible, pray and serve. But mentoring is much less formal. It's not to be a dependent relationship, but simply a friendship as you spend time with a woman who is further down the road, at least in some areas of her Christian life."[3]

Dependency on the Lord Jesus Christ alone is our goal in any discipling relationship. Discipling is not one person *over* another as much as one person coming alongside another—instructing, always supporting, and continually encouraging. Actually, a balance between structured and unstructured times with another is ideal.

Lucibel Van Atta writes in her book *Women Encouraging Women,* "Mentoring requires no special talent or God-given quality. All God asks (in His Word) is for us to take seriously the task of nurturing and building up women."[4]

Now that we have defined the word *discipleship* and identified the goal in pursuing it, how do we do it?

One-on-One Discipling

Most structured discipling falls into two categories: one-on-one or small-group meetings. First, we look at the one-on-one discipling methods. Prayerfully ask God if there is someone in your life with whom he wants you to meet regularly for a time of fellowship and Bible exploration.

Has anyone called you with a problem recently, expressing a need for fellowship or desire to learn more about the Bible? Pray first, and if you believe the Holy Spirit is giving you the go-ahead, ask that person to meet with you weekly for Bible study and discussion.

At first, plan to meet on an informal basis at least once a month to enjoy a mutual activity such as tennis, shopping, visiting a friend or sightseeing. By doing this, you are committing yourself to building a relationship and becoming a genuine friend.

A word of warning: Beware of a condescending attitude. Although your desire is to see this person grow spiritually, you, too, will have an opportunity for spiritual growth and discovery of God's Word. Remember that you are "coming alongside of" and not "standing above."

We'll assume your new friend willingly agrees to meet with you. How will you structure your time together? Sensitivity to the Holy Spirit is the key. He alone knows your friend's needs, situations, and concerns.

When beginning to disciple, determine the areas you hope to encourage a friend to pursue in her growth toward spiritual maturity. If your new friend is experiencing a crisis in her life, a study of the characteristics of God will encourage her to place her security in God as she draws near him and desires to trust him completely.

Whether she is a new Christian or searching, the Gospel of Mark could be a good beginning. Mark wrote his Gospel for the Gentiles. It is full of action and clearly portrays the person of Jesus Christ. Or you might start with the study of faith.

Faith as it is seen in the lives of biblical characters may be used to lay a foundation for the assurance of salvation. The following faith study materials are written and used by Jan Harper of Richmond, Indiana, for both one-on-one and small-group discipleship of new believers.

A Study of Faith

"Take up the shield of faith, with which you can extinguish all the flaming arrows of the evil one" (Eph. 6:16).

"And without faith it is impossible to please God" (Heb. 11:6).

What Is Faith?

(Heb. 11:1, 2 Cor. 4:18; 5:7)

After studying and praying for an understanding of these three verses, write in your own words what faith is. (You may use dictionaries, commentaries, thesaurus, and other resources. You may add other verses if you need to.)

• We are *saved* through faith (Eph. 2:8). What is the outcome of faith? (1 Pet. 1:9). How can a person obtain faith?

(Rom. 10:17). How can we have a part in helping others acquire this faith? (Rom. 10:13–15).

• We are *justified* (made righteous) by faith (Rom. 3:21–31). What provision did God make so that we might be made righteous? (Acts 13:37–39).

We are not justified by works of the law (Gal. 2:16). Does faith annul the laws that God gave to Old Testament believers? What is the relationship of faith to the law? (Rom. 3:31).

If Christ had not died and risen, our faith would be in vain (1 Cor. 15:13–19). Can you explain how the faith of our Old Testament forefathers would have also been in vain if Jesus had not died and risen?

Consider the results of justification by faith (Rom. 5:1–5). We have peace with God: (1) access to God's grace, (2) rejoice in the hope of God's glory, and (3) glory in tribulations.

• Why should we glory in tribulations? Refer to James 1:2–6.

• Limited faith is controlled by circumstances and motivated by fear of failure (Matt. 14:23–32). What happened in verse 30 to try Peter's faith?

What did Jesus do? (v. 31). What did Jesus ask? (v. 31). What does Matthew 13:58 tell us about Jesus' attitude toward lack of faith?

Why is it bad *not* to have faith? (Rom. 14:23).

• Desire for increased faith (Luke 17:5–6; Matt. 17:14–21)—What promise did Jesus give to his disciples?

What promise did Jesus give to the father? (Mark 9:20–27). What did the father reply? (v. 24).

We should also desire to increase our faith. How can we do it? (Rom. 10:17).

According to the following verses, what did we receive by faith? (Rom. 5:1–5; Eph. 3:17; Gal. 3:2, 5; 5:22; 1 Cor. 12:9).

• Great faith—Why did Jesus marvel at the centurion? (Matt. 8:5–13). Why was the woman healed? (Matt. 9:20–22). Why were the disciples able to heal the lame man? (Acts 3:1–16). Why did Paul heal the man before the man asked to be healed? (Acts 14:8–10).

• The prayer of faith—What did Jesus do for Peter? (Luke 22:31). What did Jesus tell Peter to do? What power does the prayer of faith have? (James 5:15). When we pray, what must we do in order to receive what we ask for? (Mark 11:20–26).

Along with this study, listening to tapes on faith is a fruitful exercise. Many excellent ones are available in Christian bookstores.

After completing the study sheet, read Hebrews 11 together, listing the names of great men and women of the faith. Choose Abraham, Jeremiah, Paul and Silas, Job, Enoch, or so forth to study. Give the women the Scripture references where the stories of these lives are recorded.

Finally, ask the women to answer the following questions about each person. In a small group, each is asked to come prepared to teach the others what they learned about faith through the lives of the ones they examined.

The thoughts and questions to be answered are: (1) Be able to describe the situation that the biblical character was in and tell the outcome. (2) Which of the following verses best describes the person's walk of faith? Why?

"The righteous will live by faith" (Rom. 1:17).

"We live by faith, not by sight" (2 Cor. 5:7).

"Your faith [might] not rest on men's wisdom, but on God's power" (1 Cor. 2:5).

"Faith without deeds is dead" (James 2:26).

Many books have been written to help with inductive Bible studies. These can be found in Christian bookstores. Each person could read and study a chapter. From these discuss one biblical truth that God has taught each person during her daily time with him that week.

Another goal may be to explore one theme while reading the Bible throughout the year. One friend can be studying the same theme but not as extensively. Your partner can tell you what she has learned in her personal quiet time during the week, and you can do the same for her.

Mike and Cindy McDowell, New England pastor and his wife, stress that to equip an individual for a leadership ministry, it's essential that the student develop a consistent prayer life; establish the lordship of Jesus Christ in daily decisions; and study Scriptures and enjoy a daily quiet time, as well as learn to apply biblical truth to contemporary issues. In this way she will become dependent on the power of the indwelling Holy Spirit and discover her spiritual gifts.

When you meet each week, begin with prayer, asking God to guide your discussion. Talk with one another about the Scriptures you studied that week; then take time to share prayer requests and pray for one another before leaving. Be accountable to one another to memorize a Bible verse weekly. This is also an important part of discipling. God's Word, hidden in our hearts, prepares us for life's challenges for the months and years to come.

In a survey of 250 Christian women, these recommendations were made for one-to-one discipleship:

"I have seen more growth spiritually in people's lives by getting them into the Word of God and teaching them how to study it than from using books, study guides, or devotionals." (Kim Leitch)

"I find discipling requires investing my life sacrificially in someone else, just as Christ invested his life in me." (Sandra Fullington)

"I was discipled in college by a fellow student; we studied the Bible together. She taught me to have a daily quiet time and about the indwelling Spirit and God's character. She focused on his concern for me as an individual. I am at present discipling a friend. I presented her with a Bible and a devotional book. We eat lunch together once a week and discuss problems and Christian solutions to them. We pray!" (Rose Marie McNeill)

"Weekly meetings, one on one, to share and *pray* held the greatest blessing for me. The constant, regular prayer time together, using Scriptures to praise God and encourage one another, was more important than the Bible study materials used."
(Anne Neikirt)

"I disciple using a weekly Bible study on relevant issues such as self-esteem and commitment and include an informal meeting of racquetball during the week." (Pam Carlson)

"Studies are great and *needful* to know God's Word better, but truly *being* a friend is how discipling is best taught." (Carla Cfird)

"In a mutual accountability-type relationship, a friend and I met weekly, studying a guide for homemakers and then discussing ideas and challenges and checking up on each other." (Dorothy Moss)

"I have discipled a couple of women. I try to be their friend first; then we memorize Scripture together, calling on the phone to talk weekly and meeting together monthly." (Marlene Kelly)

"I was discipled by a man at work during our lunch hour. He challenged me with questions, if I didn't come up with my own. I was a brand-new

Christian, and he had to take a lot of time on the basics. He challenged me to do Bible study, to join a prayer group, and to act on my newfound faith. He and his wife invited me and my husband to their home for fellowship and study in their prayer group, too. He also let me borrow books from his extensive library, and he encouraged me to find a ministry of my own. He spent over a year and a half working with me weekly in one-on-one, small prayer groups, and medium-sized fellowship settings." (Wendy O'Steen)

"I was discipled long distance. I was sent reading materials through the mail, and we wrote letters." (Meryl Freeman)

Small-Group Discipling

Now that we have seen the opportunities and benefits of one-on-one discipleship, we can look at the tremendous impact small-group discipleship can have on individuals. Maybe God is encouraging you to start a small-group discipleship program. Where do you begin?

In today's world and in some churches, big is best. We sometimes lose the personal touch in our ministry. People with genuine needs are sometimes lost in the crowd or fall through the cracks in the local church setting. Small-group discipleship is an effective way to minister to each person while building a strong, fellowship bond throughout the church body.

Perhaps you have thought of forming a small-group meeting in your neighborhood to reach out to women who seem lonely, isolated, or in need of Christian companionship.

Again, Lucibel Van Atta tells us, "Small-group discipling can be an especially effective and encouraging way of nurturing women. Both older and younger women may feel less threatened in a love knot of three to six. The focus seems less concentrated on any one person and greater amount of sharing usually materializes."[5]

At times friends express a simple need for fellowship and accountability to help reach the spiritual goals of daily time with God. They may want help in developing a consistent prayer life. Small groups can do this effectively.

Last summer, when the church-organized, women's weekly Bible study disbanded for the summer, four of us decided to meet throughout these months. Prayer was our focus. Using a book about devotion to God, we began each meeting with worship in prayer and the singing of Scripture choruses.

Then we discussed a chapter of the book that each of us read prior to the meeting. We shared prayer requests and prayed before closing. We not only grew closer as Christian friends, but the meetings gave a needed continuity to our summer.

It is always best when beginning a small-group ministry in the church to open it to the congregation. Everyone should feel welcome, avoiding the appearance of group cliques. You might place a notice in the Sunday bulletin asking interested people to meet on a specific day. On that day, the purpose, format, and logistics of the small-group ministry are explained.

Each interested individual is asked to make a commitment, indicating her willingness to attend regularly for a specific period of time (usually one year). She agrees to prepare faithfully for each meeting. Many times these groups are called covenant groups because of this commitment. Building relationships is essential in effective small-group ministry. Sporadic attendance and a lackadaisical attitude discourage others. Commitment is the key.

Small groups are effective when interests, needs, and desires of the members are considered. One group of new Christians may pursue a study of the basics of faith. Another might be concerned with helping members overcome grief. Still another may develop methods for local or world evangelism.

Meeting in small groups, the women in one church in Colorado Springs, Colorado, came together in the church and in homes to study the following topics:

- A verse-by-verse study of Psalms to encourage members to greater obedience and to learn to apply the truths in a specific way in their personal walk.
- A study of The Song of Songs to find God's guidelines for more loving relationships in their marriages.
- A study of the Book of Colossians to see the truth of the Word contrasted with humanist ideas and philosophies.
- A study of the character of God.
- A study using a positive resource to help members respond to the biblical directive to be Christ in the world, seeking answers to the questions of how Christians should grieve and what the Bible teaches about death and eternal life.

- A study called "Free to Be Thin," which focuses on obedience and not weight loss, using encouragement and prayer to show that eating right is a by-product of victory in many areas of life.
- A study of the name of God as each reveals God's character.
- A Bible study on prayer, searching for growth in understanding the depth of communication with God available through prayer.
- Small-group Bible studies of 1 Peter and Proverbs.
- A study of the responsibilities of marriage partners in learning to depend on God for needs rather than reducing marriage to a mutually manipulative relationship.

Discipling is an exciting aspect of the Christian life. Whatever our circumstances, God can use us to reach others for Christ. It is an opportunity to take up Christ's cross by giving of ourselves while reaping the benefits of a shared relationship and friendship. Following are comments made by women who have been members of a small-group discipleship.

> "Small groups have been an important part of my spiritual life since I was twenty-one years old (exactly forty years ago!) The warm bond that develops in these small groups that meet monthly to study Scripture and enjoy fellowship is close, meaningful, and lasting. Seven years ago when I lost my husband, one small group became my true family." (Anita Hartley)

"I am held accountable in the body of Christ by two special friends in whose life I see Jesus. They share his Word, their joys and struggles, and the love of Christ is lived out in all they do and say." (Pat Mills)

"I lead a discipleship and training ministry. The training course includes three months studying discipleship methods; then the student disciples someone in a one-on-one situation after completing the three-month study." (Anonymous)

"Recently I had a covenant group meeting in my home in which I discipled several young Christian women. We met weekly to study, worship, pray, share, and build relationships and accountability." (Anonymous)

"Three ladies meet every Wednesday for prayer and Bible study. Even though we are all involved in other studies, we treasure this time to share our lives and concerns, encouraging one another and being held accountable." (Diane Busing)

Beth Mainhood, in her book *Reaching Your World*, writes, "Discipline is not an abstract theory or a spiritual board game. It is a personal vision for how to help an individual develop her unique spiritual potential. But every personal vision requires a tailor-made practical plan."[6]

Have you considered this possibility in your life? Prayerfully ask God now if this is his plan for ministry in and through you. Use the tips in this chapter to structure and begin your own exciting adventure with God through discipleship.

Chapter 4

WOMEN AND HOSPITALITY: REFLECTING CHRIST IN YOUR HOME

THE DOORBELL RANG. I opened the door to the stifling August heat of Texas. For a brief moment I was again thankful for our air-conditioned home. Facing me was a young man, beads of perspiration covering his face. He attempted a fake salesman smile and began his prepared speech about the Bible he held in his hand.

After a moment of listening, I suggested he return later, after my husband came home from work. His dejected response touched me as I watched him lift the heavy load of books and trudge off to the next disinterested housewife.

Later, when my husband saw I had set an extra place at the table, he quizzed, "Who's coming to dinner?"

"A stranger," I said.

"A stranger? Who?" he asked.

I told him about the weary college student selling books during summer vacation to pay for his tuition fees. We agreed to invite him to dinner if he returned.

In a few minutes a knock sounded at the door. "Won't you come in?" I asked, smiling. "I don't know your name, but my husband and I would like you to join us for dinner."

He was incredulous. "Do you mean it?" he said, hesitating.

"Sure," I said.

With a wide smile my husband welcomed him and said, "As Christians, we think it's what Jesus would do. My wife noticed how tired you seemed."

The evening that followed was one of ministry. The boy wanted to return home to be with his family, but his boss had made him feel guilty by calling him a quitter.

After a lengthy conversation my husband encouraged him to go home and find a job there. The boy left and seemed comforted and encouraged.

Weeks later a thank-you note arrived in the mail. The instant impulse to invite a stranger to dinner resulted in the boy coming to a personal faith in Christ. God's plan was fulfilled.

What is hospitality? The Greek word *philoxenia* tells much about its original function. *Philo* refers to brotherly love; *xeno* means strangers. Combine the two and you have "love of strangers."

Over and again we see Old Testament directives toward hospitality. In Leviticus 23:22 we read, "When you reap the harvest of your land, do not reap to the very edges of your field or gather the gleanings of your harvest. Leave them for the poor and alien. I am the LORD your God."

Again, in Isaiah 58:6–9, God speaks:

> Is not this the kind of fasting I have chosen: to loose the chains of injustice and untie the cords of the yoke, to set the oppressed free and break every yoke? Is it not to share your food with the hungry and to provide the poor wanderer with shelter—when you see the naked, to clothe him, and not to turn away from your own flesh and blood?

> Then your light will break forth like the dawn, and your healing will quickly appear; then your right-eousness will go before you, and the glory of the LORD will be your rear guard. Then you will call, and the LORD will answer; you will cry for help, and he will say: Here am I.

This act of hospitality was a sacred duty throughout Israelite history and continued to be seen as such by the early Christians.

In a letter to the king written by the second-century pagan, Aristides, we read his description of the Christian activity of that time: "When they see a stranger, they take him into their homes and rejoice over him as a very brother . . . and if they hear that one of their number is imprisoned or afflicted on account of the name of their Messiah, all of them anxiously minister to his necessity.

"If there is among them any that is poor and needy, and if they have no spare food, they fast two or three days in order to supply to the needy their lack of food. They observe the precepts of their Messiah with much care, living justly and soberly as the Lord their God commanded them."[1]

A young woman recently questioned me at a conference, "What has happened to hospitality today?" I thought about her words later. *What has happened to hospitality?* I wondered. In our culture with its busy lifestyle and "home on display" mind-set, we have lost the joy found in the simple thoughtfulness of extending hospitality.

Many women with whom I've spoken feel that they don't know how to be hospitable, while others complain that they don't have time. Is it because we have replaced the warmth of hospitality with the burden of elaborate entertaining?

Many of the books I have read describe hospitality as a gift. Some people have it and some don't, they say. But in my study of Scripture, hospitality appears to be a command for all Christians.

Peter wrote, "Offer hospitality to one another without grumbling" (1 Pet. 4:9). The overseer, or pastor today, is to be hospitable (1 Tim. 3:2; Titus 1:8). As women, we are all to "share with God's people who are in need. Practice hospitality" (Rom. 12:13), and not neglect to show hospitality to strangers (1 Tim. 5:10; Heb. 13:2).

Do you notice the person who sits next to you in the pew each Sunday morning? He or she could be your stranger. Unfortunately much of society's exclusiveness has pervaded the church. Often there are cliques, those who are members of small, inside groups and those who are on the outside.

Younger women may ignore older ones at meetings, or older exclude younger women. Both young and older women attending a Bible study may be excluded because they had not attended earlier sessions. Well-dressed women may disregard those who wear plainer, less-expensive clothing. Longtime members of a congregation may ignore the visitor, the new members, the single parent, or the young teen.

"The community of faith is not some exclusive club sitting on the edge of society and scrutinizing potential worshippers," writes Ruth Senter. "Christians have the privilege, as believers in Jesus Christ, to break these habits of elitism and snobbery. We can begin obeying Christ's clear commands about hospitality."[2]

Jesus reminds us, "And if anyone gives a cup of cold water to one of these little ones because he is my disciple, I tell you the truth, he will certainly not lose his reward" (Matt. 10:42).

June Curtis compares entertainment and hospitality in her article "A Plate of Warm Cookies." She says, "When we entertain, we (may) feel as though we are on center stage having to do a song and dance routine. That is, everything must be perfect, down to having every weed pulled in the yard and finding not one speck of dust any place." On the other hand, "in gracious hospitality, love is the most important ingredient, not a perfect house or yard or even perfect children," she concludes.[3]

Where Do You Begin?

To avoid succumbing to the pressure of perfection, there are ways you can extend hospitality to others without panicking.

Keep it simple. Coffee and a cupcake offered with a warm smile can go a long way. An invitation for dessert and coffee is usually easy to prepare and can result in a relaxing break for both the hostess and the guest. If you're planning a meal, choose a menu you can prepare with ease, one you've prepared before and feel will guarantee a tasty, successful meal.

Plan ahead. Keep a favorite casserole in the freezer, one you are ready to offer unexpected guests. A sliced, frozen loaf of French bread topped with pizza sauce, browned beef, and cheese accompanied by a simple salad can provide a quick, flavorful meal.

Consider eye appeal. If all you have is tea, serve it in a china teapot. A single flower or a rosebud in a vase on the table shows warmth.

Involve guests. Whenever a guest offers to help, give him a job. Simple tasks remove awkward moments.

Serve what people like. It's not necessary to try to prepare a gourmet creation that may be returned to the kitchen untouched. Keep it tasty but simple.

Rest thirty minutes before guests arrive. Find time to sit down, relax, and pray that God's perfect will will be accomplished through the occasion.

Keep a small notebook of easy menu plans. List a few quick meals that have proven successful. If you entertain frequently, record the names of the guests and the menus served in order to avoid repetition.

Barbara Barker of Birmingham, Alabama, defines Christian hospitality as focusing on the needs of others, bringing them into your life where you can minister to them and love them, and where you can demonstrate the sufficiency and love of God. "God is not interested in seeing us, what *we* can do, who *we* are," she remarks. "God wants to see the reality of Jesus in us, the power and sufficiency of Jesus in us that is going to draw the world to him, to exalt him and lift him up."[4]

Whom Do You Invite?

Start with your guest list by identifying the needs of those around you. Whom do you feel God most wants you to reach out to? Alexa Ketchum of Louisville, Texas, asks, "Where does your compassion lead you? Does it lead you to that divorced woman who struggles with the responsibility of rearing her children alone? Are you led to those little children in your neighborhood who don't attend church or don't know about the Lord?"

Have you considered the visitors or church members whom you see often but barely know? Mary Edith Huggins of Nashville, Tennessee, has captured the essence of the hospitality ministry. A gracious woman, she and her husband expand this ministry of caring through prayer. They pray first for God's leading to individuals with needs and problems. Often these prove to be both strangers and friends.

Then, after inviting the individual for dinner or dessert, they tell them, "If you want to talk, we are here to listen. If you want to pray, we are here to pray. If you want to leave and forget your problem, we won't even mention it."

Their home is offered as a place of solace and refuge where each person receives the ministry they most desire. Mary Edith encourages women to be vulnerable. "Raise the windows of your soul so someone can peek in, and through your caring, find comfort," she tells them.

"Unpack the word *hospitality*," writes Texan John Ragland, "and you find the word *hospital*. We live in a society and culture filled with injured and hurting people. God has called you to himself and given you beautiful homes and families so you can minister to injured and hurting people. God wants your home to be a hospital where people can discover the only One who puts things back together again."[5]

After identifying those around you to whom God might want you to minister, consider how you as a Christian woman can lead your church into more meaningful participation in a hospitality ministry. Even though you may not be aware of it, the opportunities are plentiful.

Frank Barker, a pastor in Birmingham, Alabama, writes, "If someone doesn't build relationships within the first six to eight months they are in your church, you will usually lose them. Small groups in homes where you create a warm atmosphere not possible in a church building will help prevent them from leaving through the back door."[6]

Two hundred and fifty women were asked to describe one successful method or program which furthered the ministry of hospitality in their personal life, church, or community. They were asked to describe the organization and implementation. These are their suggestions.

Visitor's dinners–A volunteer group took turns inviting newcomers home for Sunday dinner.–Mary Lou Seal

Saltshaker program–Three or four couples met for dinner (each couple was responsible for part of the meal); then the next month the groups were "shaken" for a meal with different couples. One person organized the groups.–Gini Love

Knife and fork dinners—A host and one church family invite two visiting couples to dinner on the first Saturday of each month.

"Guess who's coming to dinner" mystery dinners—Hosts and guests signed up on an available sign-up sheet. The families were secretly matched. The hosts were given only the number of guests who would be attending and guests were given only the host's address. These proved to be a great surprise.

Hospitality coordinator—Assign a person who keeps up with needs in the church and contacts the proper groups to meet these needs, such as organizing meals for a new mother or the family of a sick member.

Couples dinner—Divide the church up into fours (two couples) and ask them to do something together each month for three months (or as often as they like). After three months the couples are reassigned.—Wendy O'Steen

Dinner party format—Three couples invited eight to ten couples for a dinner party. Included were both new and longtime members of the church. They had cookouts, formal dinner parties, or pool parties but *no* covered dish. They wanted to treat these couples to a special evening. They usually played games after dinner.—Allyson Bentwell

Conversational dinners—Interested persons in the church signed up to participate. Singles were paired and included with married couples. From October through May each pair was assigned to six other people to share dinner that month. During the eight-month period, each pair served as hosts twice, inviting the other six into their home. Each couple agreed to supply a salad, a dessert, or a vegetable dish. (This works well on a four-month basis too.)

Philadelphia dinners—The church family is divided into small groups to meet three or four times a year for informal dinners in many homes on the same night. Host families volunteer to serve the dinner in their homes. Using a theme—Mexican, Chinese, French, and so forth—each person brings food to share.

Prayer dinners—Lynn Erickson writes, "My husband and I pray during the week for the Lord to provide someone for us to bring home for lunch after church service. It is always a great blessing."

Snappy cookers—For the Wednesday night church suppers, eight crews of five women became the Snappy Cookers. Each crew had a crew chief who was responsible for planning the meal and instructing the crew. Each crew cooked once every two months. The program grew beyond manageable numbers; so they are now considering hiring a person to oversee the program, plan the meals, coordinate the buying, and take care of the kitchen. However, the weekly crews would continue to help cook and serve.

An added benefit happened when the women who cook together developed friendship bonds. Their husbands often served, and the food quality improved. The pastor served the dessert from a cart so that he was able to fellowship with members.—Pat Kleinknecht

College friendships—We invite college students to supper each week before an evening class.—Teal Mitchell

Meeters, greeters, and feeders—One church stations three people in the church each Sunday to meet visitors. The first person meets the individual at the door; the second stands inside the foyer to greet and talk with the individual. A final person comes prepared to invite the visitor for dinner after the service.

Football Super Bowl—The congregation is divided into groups of eight to ten. A volunteer leader is chosen for each group. The names in each group are listed on a slip of paper with the leader's name at the beginning and end of the list. Each slip is glued to one side of a brown football made out of cardboard or poster board.

Beginning and ending with the leader, the football is passed from one person on the list to the next. Each person visits the next person on the list, passing on the football. Visits can include small gifts of food, invitation to dinner, and so forth. The passing of the football ends with a congregational Super Bowl potluck dinner. (Couples are usually paired when making the lists.)

Small-church hospitality—To make sure each member has an opportunity to be in our home each month, we invite those who wish to come to join us for a covered-dish dinner the last Sunday of each month.—Bonnie Conard

Evangelistic dinners—We had a monthly covered-dish dinner in homes with a speaker or speaking couple who gave testimony of God's work in their lives. This was a community-wide group. Friends, neighbors, and newcomers were invited. Several came to know the Lord through this ministry.

Morning coffee and luncheon program—Once a week the church hosted a morning coffee with a speaker and program. For working women a luncheon and program were also prepared.

Offering plate get-together—Everyone who wanted to participate wrote their name, address, and phone number on a slip of paper and dropped it in the offering plate. At the end of the service, members withdrew a slip and took responsibility for showing some type of hospitality to the person whose name was on the slip.–Karen Crocker

Dessert and coffee–Busy mothers invite church members for dessert and coffee or "make your own sundae" get-togethers.

Once-a-month date–We invite the couples in our Sunday school class to a monthly evening out. We set up card tables with tablecloths throughout the house for the covered-dish meal. Then one couple talks about God's work in their lives and marriage.–Fran Sandin

Breadwinner ministry–Following a visitor's first visit to the church, a loaf of homemade bread is taken to their home by a church member.

Evening socials–We formed a committee to plan and implement different activities each month for church participation. The most successful have been a bowling night, ice-cream social with games, a picnic, and covered-dish dinners for returning students who attend the church.

Guest cottage–"My husband and I built a guest cottage for visiting missionaries. We have committed our home and hospitality to the Lord, for it's all his."–Mary Van Puffels

Missionary hospitality team–Host families volunteer to have furloughing or traveling missionaries in their homes.

Pairs and spares–Monthly night-out dinner and fellowship for couples and singles.–Evelyn Sno

International hospitality–We sponsor international students attending the university and invite them for meals, sightseeing, and church dinners.–Charlene Yunker

Crisis shepherding–This provides housing and care for pregnant teenagers who await the birth and adoption of their babies.

Game night–Everyone brings their favorite game. Each person chooses a game table and plays for thirty minutes, then moves to another table and group. Good mixer for young and old.

Need-meeting hospitality–Hospitality planned around needs of members of the congregation. Dinners are prepared and delivered to a home, an afternoon of babysitting is provided for mothers, notes of encouragement are written, the ill are visited, and their houses cleaned. Transportation is provided for elderly church members.

Burden bearing–Care for a bereaved person after a week or so when they are alone and visitors no longer come by, including them in family activities, inviting them to lunch, visiting them, and listening if they wish to talk. Help with household repairs and chores.

Although suggestions for hospitality are endless, at least one of the above may provide a springboard for you so that you, too, can follow Jesus' example and reach out with compassion to those around you.

Jo Anne Reed of St. Louis writes, "My ministry of hospitality was greatly improved when I began praying for a servant's heart. I began to ask for God's strength to serve others in joy and to give entertainment of others to Jesus so that he would be glorified in my home.

"Committing your home to the Lord for his use in hospitality opens up exciting new experiences with God and his people. You become his instrument for ministry and change in other's lives. Your home first becomes a refuge for your husband and children and then a place of healing for those who hurt."

It is said that a woman determines the atmosphere of her home. Is yours one where God is loved and his Word studied daily? Has your home been completely dedicated to God for his plans and purposes? Is gracious hospitality available without anxiety or apology?

In her article "Breaking Bread with the World" Martha Chamberlain writes,

> Two of Jesus' followers fled Jerusalem early on Easter morning after the cataclysmic events of that weekend—and a magnificent awakening occurred as they sat down to break bread with the Stranger.
>
> Was it by accident that, as Jesus took a small loaf of bread, and broke it, and was passing it to them, that a miracle ensued? The moment was electric—their eyes were opened. He had been there all along, but it was through their hospitality, in their open home, and the breaking of bread together, that the Stranger became Christ among them.[7]

This, too, is your opportunity to follow Jesus' example of hospitality, offered to his disciples and to you.

Chapter 5

DESIGNING A WOMEN'S CONFERENCE

*I awaken early and quickly begin to dress, hoping that
I will not disturb my husband and sleeping children. As
I slip outside the motel-room door into the crisp morning
air, the bird calls fill the air. I silently thank the Lord that
this lovely East Texas town was chosen to host the much-
anticipated Annual Spring Women's Conference.*

*Bowing my head, I pray, "Praise, glory, and honor
belong to you, Father. Today many women come with
burdens, cares, hurts, and anxieties. Open their hearts.
Make them fallow ground for planting the seeds of your
presence and purpose. Take this day, and use it to your
glory. In Jesus' name, Amen."*

Quietly I relive the hours of preparation that made this moment possible. My desire has always been to see lives changed by God. The privilege of being used by him as an instrument to perform his work make the days exciting and worthwhile. Today I anticipate its fulfillment joyfully. (Excerpt from my personal journal dated April 25, 1987.)

HAVE YOU EVER THOUGHT that planning a special conference or retreat is a way to discover the needs of women as well as a way to look for avenues to meet those needs?

Like most of us, I was first overwhelmed at the thought of planning a conference that would reach one hundred women or more. Now, after many years' experience in designing and directing women's programs, I have developed guidelines to simplify the planning so that under God's direction any woman can easily accomplish it. These guidelines are formulated to equip you to be confident as you plan a successful meeting. Adjust them for your specific situation and allow God to use you in identifying and meeting the needs of the women he has placed in your life.

Guidelines for Planning a Conference

Pray. Any project must begin and end with prayer. Remember Jesus said, "Apart from me you can do nothing" (John 15:5). Ask the Lord to direct your thoughts and plans so that you properly develop the program.

Find a prayer partner or group who will commit themselves to designated times of prayer. Ask them to pray that God will bring together the women whom he wants to attend and that he will prepare their hearts to hear his voice through all the activities and teaching of his Word.

Organize a program committee. First, telephone anyone who has expressed interest in a women's seminar or speaker. Ask them if they would be interested in helping to plan a women's conference. You can also prepare a simple questionnaire to poll additional interest from women in your local church. Also ask friends for the names of their acquaintances whom they think would be interested.

After speaking with these women, invite them to attend a planning meeting in your home. Include those who have attended previous conferences and ask them to be resource persons as you search for fresh ideas. The first meeting might include lunch or brunch as a get-acquainted session.

Begin with prayer. Ask God to direct your efforts so that you will be able to outline your purpose and goals and in order to plan a dynamic, spiritual conference. Pray that all will be sensitive to his will for that special day or weekend.

Outline goals and objectives. As the hostess, come to this first meeting with suggestions for goals and objectives for the conference. Be ready to present them to the program committee. First, establish the need for the conference. In a few sentences write the purpose you feel this conference will serve. The primary goal of any Christian conference should be to minister to the needs of others. But what are the needs of those who will attend your conference? To determine this, ask yourself, "In what area are the women hurting and in need of encouragement?"

Next decide on your focus. "Will it be geared to equip participants for more effective teaching? Evangelism? Or perhaps a hospitality ministry? Would the personal testimony of one main speaker who has known God's faithfulness in the midst of trial and suffering be most meaningful? Or would the exploration of one topic through a small-group workshop be more effective?"

Establish the format. The key to a successful conference schedule is variety. Genuine, life-changing ministry can be hindered by long-winded lectures or boring business meetings. Choose a varied and interesting format.

Whether you are planning a one-day conference, weekend retreat, weeklong seminar, or one-hour program, formats are many. Most fit into the five following categories, which focus on:

Keynote speaker—All activities are chosen to support a well-known authority or speaker's address or seminar.

Topic speakers—You might plan to focus on a primary subject in a one-day conference. If the theme is encouragement, for example, several speakers could address different aspects of the subject. Titles might include: Personal Encouragement Found in the Bible, Encouraging Your Husband, Encouraging Your Children, The Ministry of Encouragement in the Church, and so forth.

Workshop—Using one essential theme, several workshop leaders can introduce a variety of subjects. This format allows a hands-on approach. Those attending actually participate in the discussion or craft projects. Written handouts can be distributed to take home, share with others, or use later.

Small-group directed study—This conference divides the women into small groups, which have previously selected leaders. A variety of subjects relating to women can be explored from a biblical perspective. Using an inductive Bible study method, prepare a question-and-answer sheet. Ask women to find Bible verses relating to a particular subject, answer questions, and then participate in a small-group discussion. Some of the subjects to be covered could include: God's Design for Biblical Parenting, Widowhood: Conquering Loneliness, On Being a Single Parent, or Dealing with Adversity (job loss, family crisis, and so forth).

The following formats could be used as an example.

Workshop Format

Theme: A Woman and Her Home

8:45–9:30 a.m.	Refreshments and Get-Acquainted Time
9:30–9:40 a.m.	Welcome and Introduction to the Day's Activities
9:40–10:30 a.m.	"Hospitality: Reflecting Christ in Your Home"
	Sheets are distributed listing ideas for planning small-group Bible studies, dinners for ministry to

couples, hosting missionaries in your home, neighborhood coffees, and so forth. Discussion follows with opportunities to share personal experiences in regard to the ministry of hospitality.

10:30–10:40 a.m.	Break
10:40–11:30 a.m.	"Personal Time Management: Try a Notebook"

Materials are provided which help women put order into their daily lives. Personal organizational skills are described, and time for discussion is allotted for helpful tips from the group.

11:30–12:00 p.m.	Discussion period in regard to previous workshops
12:00–1:00 p.m.	Lunch
1:00–1:50 p.m.	"Creative Activities for Family Worship"

Ideas for creative family worship and the special celebration of holidays are provided. Actual crafts made by families in preparation for a holiday or visual aids of any kind are displayed. Instructions are given so others can duplicate these items.

1:50–2:00 p.m.	Closing

Combined lecture and workshop format—A main speaker addresses the group; then small groups are formed for interaction and discussion. The following is an example of such a format.

Combined Lecture and Workshop Format

Theme: Being Christ's Body

10:00 a.m.   Arrival

Fellowship and coffee (Time for visiting informally.)

Sing familiar choruses interspersed with coordinated Scriptures.

Keynote speaker: "Building Up One Another in Love" (God's church, Christ's body)

12:00 p.m.   Lunch

1:00 p.m.   Small-group workshops. Groups rotate after each twenty-five-minute segment so that women attend each workshop.

"Leading Christ's Body in Worship"—Verses of Scripture are set to music, designed to keep the Word of God in a woman's heart as she goes about her tasks each day. Scripture readings are interspersed. Guitar music may be used for instruction. Printed information sheets are used. Scriptures are identified.

"Tips for Meeting Nursery Needs"—Sharing insights about finding volunteer and paid workers, planning lessons that meet children's needs, presenting ideas for introducing toddlers to God and the Bible, and discovering efficiency in operation and equipment.

"Hispanic Ministry in Texas"—Scripture: "I am the bread of life" (John 6:48). Use a poster of the state with Hispanic churches marked. Distribute Spanish copies of the Gospel of John and Spanish tracts for evangelism. Have special music with guitar and Spanish gospel music. Demonstrate making a flour tortilla. Provide a printed recipe handout.

2:30 p.m.   Closing Hymn and Dismissal

Sample: Small-Group Discussion Sheet

Are you a joyful woman? Jesus intends for you to experience joy. Jesus spoke these words to his Father before his crucifixion and resurrection: "I am coming to you now, but I say these things while I am still in the world, so that they [believers in Christ] may have the full measure of my joy within them" (John 17:13 HCSB).

Find verses 9–11 of John 15 and write Jesus' words concerning joy. When was the last time you felt genuine joy?

What caused your joyful feelings?

The Psalms are filled with references to joy. Find the following verses and discuss the writer's cause for joy: Psalm 16:11 (*God's presence brings joy*); Psalm 28:7 (*God's help brings joy*); Psalm 43:4 (*Recognizing God's person brings joy*); Psalm 51:12 (*God's salvation brings joy*); Psalm 92:4 (*God's deeds bring joy*); and Psalm 94:19 (*God's consolation brings joy*).

Joy comes in response to whose action? (*God's*) God's activity in our life is our greatest cause for joy. What has God done in your life this week for which you can thank him? (*God enabled me to read the Bible each morning; God comforted me when a friend's criticism hurt deeply; God answered a specific prayer.*)

What can you do this week that will encourage someone else to be joyful?

After considering the above or other alternatives, outline your purpose and goals and then choose the format you believe would be most interesting and stimulating to the particular group.

Determine the time schedule. As you and others continue to talk, agree on a time that will help assure a good attendance. Many working women are unable to attend workshops during the week. Others may not drive at night. Select a time when the most women can participate.

Next, select a date based on participants' convenience. A committee should be selected to determine location and the availability of hotels or other meeting facilities, cost of food and other provisions. This information should be submitted to the program committee several days prior to their next meeting for discussion, evaluation, and decision-making.

Decide on a conference schedule. This will be one of your most important decisions. Kathy Cheeley of Birmingham, Alabama, an experienced conference director, suggests the following format possibilities:

One-Day Meeting—General Format

9:30 a.m.	Registration with refreshment table
10:00 a.m.	Get acquainted activity or game
10:30 a.m.	Welcome and introducing speaker
10:40 a.m.	Guest speaker

11:15 a.m.	Informal segment (movie, slides, skit, question/answer, music, and so forth)
12:00 p.m.	Business if necessary—keep it brief. (Type and distribute as much information as possible rather than having extensive reading of minutes, treasurer's report, and so forth.)
12:30 p.m.	Lunch
1:30 p.m.	Sing-along (Move from fun songs to more serious. The song leader you choose is important.)
2:00 p.m.	Guest speaker
3:00 p.m.	Dismiss

Overnight Retreat

5:00 p.m.	Registration
6:00 p.m.	Supper
7:00 p.m.	Fun time (games, songs, creative introductions)
8:00 p.m.	Speaker
9:15 p.m.	Sharing and prayer time (Separate into small groups or meet together, depending on size.)
10:00 p.m.	Bedtime

8:30 a.m.	Breakfast
9:30 a.m.	Speaker (or workshops)
10:15 a.m.	Discussion groups
11:00 a.m.	Wrap-up (Share things learned and summarize theme accomplished.)
11:45 a.m.	Lunch and dismissal

One-Day Meeting Seminar Format

9:30 a.m.	Welcome
9:35 a.m.	Personal testimony on the subject relating to speaker's focus
10:00 a.m.	Break (for women to stand up and stretch)
10:10 a.m.	Seminar 1—guest speaker
10:45 a.m.	Special Music
10:55 a.m.	Break
11:00 a.m.	Seminar 2—guest speaker
11:45 a.m.	Lunch
12:45 p.m.	Seminar 3—guest speaker
1:15 p.m.	Informal Segment (film, slides, skit, question/answer)
2:00 p.m.	Dismiss

Weekend Retreat

Friday

5:00 p.m.	Registration begins
7:00 p.m.	Buffet dinner
8:30 p.m.	Mixer
9:00 p.m.	Music
9:15 p.m.	Meeting—keynote speaker
10:00 p.m.	Snacks

Saturday

8:30 a.m.	Breakfast
9:00 a.m.	Thought for the day
9:05 a.m.	Music
9:15 a.m.	Personal quiet time
10:15 a.m.	Meeting—keynote speaker
12:30 p.m.	Lunch
1:15 p.m.	Afternoon free time
4:00 p.m.	Possible video presentation or other planned event
4:30 p.m.	Question and answer session with keynote speaker
6:00 p.m.	Dinner
7:15 p.m.	Music
7:30 p.m.	Meeting—keynote speaker
8:30 p.m.	Break
9:00 p.m.	Snacks and talent show

Sunday

8:15 a.m.	Breakfast buffet
9:00 a.m.	Thought for the day
9:05 a.m.	Music
9:15 a.m.	Personal quiet time
10:00 a.m.	Meeting—keynote speaker
11:15 a.m.	Free time
12:30 p.m.	Lunch
1:00 p.m.	Conference concludes

Plan programs that inspire. Now that you have begun with prayer, outlined goals, established a format, and selected a schedule, the fun begins. Plan an exciting and stimulating program.

Start by choosing a theme. The possibilities are limitless. The following ideas are some I have seen used successfully.

Patterns in life–More young women seek to know how to sew, cook, and develop the home-making skills they often lack. Focus on one of these skills. With a program cover resembling a sewing pattern, information inside is printed on paper cut in pattern piece designs. Included in the day's events is a special seminar on wardrobe coordination presented by the owner of a local fabric store.

God does not need special clay to make fine china–Three women share their personal testimony about the unique gifts God developed and used in their lives to minister to others. China table settings of many patterns are provided while several women tell their unique story.

Passing the legacy—Women are provided with suggested books, written sheets, and hands-on activities that enable them to rear and disciple their children for Christ. Workshops are divided by children's age groups so that the women can attend the ones related to their child's age or choose one of particular interest.

Retreat on the life of Fanny Crosby (or another famous Christian woman)—Discover how one woman's life was used by God.

Make it your mission—A Spanish-speaking church congregation could plan a complete program to introduce their mission program. Spanish is spoken in the beginning so that the women understand how a foreign missionary feels in a country where he or she is unable to communicate with ease. Later both English and Spanish are used.

These are only a few suggestions. Create your own theme based on the activities and interests of your attendees. After choosing a theme, plan related activities to include speakers, movies, slides, skits, question-answer sessions, personal testimony, music, panel discussions, and workshops. Begin with an icebreaker game that reinforces your theme. Take this opportunity to be creative!

Contact program participants. At this time select the one who will be responsible for each aspect of the program. A member of the program committee becomes chairperson of each major area of responsibility. The areas needing guidance are:

Speaker arrangements—Coordination of program, travel arrangements, and honorarium.

Publicity for meeting—Newsletters, preregistration, name tags, registration (day of meeting), and program packets (day of meeting).

Music—Theme song or hymn, choruses, song leader, and special music.

Refreshments and decorations—Sweet breads, doughnuts, or other food, and table decorations.

When choosing a committee chairperson for each development area and assigning responsibilities, search for the people who are capable of planning and directing a God-centered seminar. After developing a list of speakers, workshop leaders, panel discussion members, and/or musicians, pray for guidance and then phone or write each one until an acceptance is granted.

Susan Hunt, previous women's ministry coordinator for the Presbyterian Church in America, suggests a six-step guideline for inviting speakers: (1) Speakers should be contacted at least three months in advance. For better known speakers a year is preferable. (2) Provide the speaker with the topic. (3) Send the program schedule indicating the length of speaking time. (4) Offer to make plane and hotel reservations, if necessary, and cover her travel expense. (5) Find out if she has a set fee for speaking. If not, ask the committee to decide on an honorarium. Inform the speaker of the amount. (6) Send a note of appreciation to her.

Designate responsibilities. Having secured speakers, you now should involve as many women as possible. When women contribute to a conference, they invest in its success and it takes on new meaning for everyone. Ask for volunteers and search out women who are known to be creative and innovative.

List needs and assign duties to volunteers. Check with them to ensure their support and enthusiastic involvement.

Eight to ten weeks before the conference date, invite volunteers to a planning session. Committee chairpersons will assign volunteers their duties. Some of these might be:

Registration–One or two women will be needed to greet and register arriving guests.

Refreshments–If coffee and pastries or doughnuts are being offered at the time of registration, women will be needed to serve them.

Name tags–Several women will be needed to design colorful and attractive name tags. Many times the theme of the conference is included in the design.

Place setting favors (optional)–If you plan to provide favors to the participants, seek out artistic and creative workers to design and construct them. Some possible examples include:

- Recipe holders–Glue brightly painted wood clothespins to a 2½ by 2½-inch piece of half inch plywood. Clip a recipe and Scripture verse to each and place at each table place setting.

- Bookmark–Cut a 2½ by 6-inch rectangle of counted cross-stitch fabric and cross-stitch a simple design on fabric. Fray the top and bottom edges a half-inch. Cut an 8-inch piece of wide grosgrain ribbon and glue to back of cross-stitch fabric.

- Personal journal–Fold 15 sheets of 8½ by 11 typing paper in half. Design a cover with heavy card stock and staple all into a small booklet. At the top of each sheet place a Bible verse or quote that highlights your conference theme. You have created a *30 Days with God Personal Quiet Time Journal* for each participant.

Table decorations—With the theme in mind, decorate tables with flowers, fruit, or original arrangements. Ask volunteering women to meet and set up tables with place settings and decorations.

Get-acquainted activity—Icebreakers are important in helping a group of strangers become acquainted. Committee volunteers plan activities, gather supplies, and conduct games.

Hosting speakers—Seek volunteers to be responsible for housing and entertaining a visiting speaker overnight. In some cases it will be necessary to offer transportation to and from the airport.

Floaters—These women direct and assist participation.

Luncheon hostesses—Assign a woman to each table and ask her to encourage discussion. (You can actually give her a list of things for the group to discuss, such as a favorite holiday memory, childhood experience, or significant person in their life.)

Publicity helpers—Prepare and mail brochures.

Create publicity that works. Now that the program is planned and your speakers committed. It is time to get the word out. A workable calendar for publicity should be used *eight weeks before the meeting.* Make a list of possible participants. Create an attractive brochure, flyer, or letter describing the event which includes the following: theme or title of conference, date, location, time, schedule of events, brief biographical glimpse of speakers, cost (if applicable), telephone number for further information, and directions to meeting place. These facts can be highlighted by adding attractive illustrations or small cartoon figures.

Include a reservation form in this mailing with requested return date (approximately two weeks before meeting). You may choose to send a stamped, self-addressed postcard as shown.

Suggested Form

Name _____

Address _____

Amount enclosed for cost of conference _____

Nursery Reservations (Please list names and ages of children attending.)

Please return reservations to:

Name _____

Address _____

Three weeks before the meeting, a final reminder could begin with words: Send Your Reservations *Today!* Guarantee interest with an attractive, eye-catching notice. Pray that the women will respond to the Holy Spirit's prompting.

Kathy Cheeley suggests the following creative publicity suggestions. Find a large refrigerator box and place it in the entry hall of the church or meeting room. Put a sign on the box which reads, "For Women Only." When women look inside the box, they see a large, bright poster announcing the upcoming conference.

Kathy also suggests filling gelatin capsules (available in any pharmacy) with a little message. The message could read, "Are you tired, run-down, need a change? Do you have the winter blues? Come to a (spring, summer, winter) luncheon."

Follow up. To verify progress, follow up on the work of the committee leaders and helpers three weeks before your conference date. Check that reservations are coming in daily. A final reminder or wrap-up is needed. Answer questions or offer help. Congratulate the workers who have given their time and efforts to help make the conference a success. Let them know you appreciate their assistance and commitment.

Prepare program materials. Many women enjoy and expect to receive a program or packet of interesting material that describes the conference events and gives something to take home for future reading, study, or use. The packet may include:

- A schedule of the day's activities
- Brochures or instructional materials
- Outlines of the speaker's message (if previously provided by speaker)
- Quiet-time suggestions (Scripture references provided to look up and think about during breaks)
- Note sheets—sheets listing seminars with empty spaces for taking notes as speakers give their presentations.
- Music choruses—typed words for a sing-along section of the program.
- Evaluation sheet—imperative for planning further conferences. The following information should be requested: (1) Please state the part of today's program you found most meaningful. (2) "A day of personal inspiration and edification" was the purpose of our conference. What did you find personally edifying and inspiring? (3) Do you have suggestions for improving

next year's conference? (4) Can you suggest future speakers, musicians, or others you would be interested in hearing?

Anticipate last-minute details. Two weeks before the date, sit down in a quiet spot and mentally walk through the conference agenda. Try to anticipate any unexpected or overlooked details. Has someone arranged for any needed sound or electronic equipment, provided tables for books, refreshments, and registration? Is there a punch bowl for the reception the evening before the conference? Are CDs and digital recorders in place? Are the volunteers prepared to do their jobs?

By rehearsing the sequence of events, you are able to eliminate some possible problems. Ask yourself if someone is prepared to introduce the speakers, offer the opening prayer, and make announcements. Review your own responsibilities; make a note of those you might forget.

By doing this preliminary evaluation, the panic of forgotten details will be eliminated.

Relinquish responsibility and relax. The long-awaited day arrives. Prayerful preparation and attention to detail have built the framework for an effective instrument for God's use. You have done your part.

Leave the rest to his sovereign control and timing. Believe that he brought those who are present and that he will accomplish his purposes according to his plan.

Relax and enjoy God's ministry in and through you. Receive from his hand those special things which he has prepared for you as well. Thank him for his provision and constant care that made this day a reality.

Express final thanks. The conference is over. It has been a great day, worth rejoicing over. Needs were met and hearts touched. God used a well-planned day for his service. For this you can be joyful.

Many people have made this success possible. You want them to know that you appreciate their help. Write a note. Express your thanks and appreciation commenting on any special effort or contribution each person has made. Be sincere.

What happened April 25? As I mentioned earlier, God used a carefully planned conference to accomplish his purpose. April 25 was a wonderful day. The Lord abundantly blessed our efforts. I sat and thanked my heavenly Father for displaying his power to us that day and for touching so many in need. I thanked him also for the privilege of being his instrument to accomplish his will.

You, too, can plan a women's conference. Do not hesitate. Use these guidelines, depend on God's help, and give it a try. It is work, but the benefits make all the effort worthwhile.

Now let's explore the most important aspect of any ministry—prayer. In the next chapter you will discover creative ways to lead women in effective prayer and help them develop a deeper trust in and dependence on God as they communicate with him.

Chapter 6

WOMEN AND EVANGELISM: WHO ME?

PLEASE TAKE THE FOLLOWING personal evangelism quiz. Write *true* or *false* beside each question.

_____ 1. I feel guilty because I don't share my faith often enough.

_____ 2. I'm afraid of what people will think if I start talking about Jesus Christ.

_____ 3. I wouldn't know how to begin an evangelism program in my church if someone asked me to.

_____ 4. I want to witness to strangers but just can't find the words.

_____ 5. Evangelism seems so difficult that I resist attempting it.

If you answered *true* to any of these questions, then this chapter is for you. We will explore evangelism on a personal level. Have you ever asked yourself why you find evangelism so difficult?

"Gallup polls show that 96 percent of Americans say they believe in God," writes Anne Marley Work. "Though many are not Christians, . . . they may be closer to an intimate understanding and appreciation of Christ than we imagine."[1]

Why do we maintain an "us and them" mentality? Every person has an inner need for Jesus Christ. There are no exceptions. This was God's intention when he created man. No matter what the person's outer appearance may project—success, wealth, independence—the basic need is there.

"While we mow the lawn or ride the subway, or eat pasta salad in a restaurant, something is happening all around us—something we don't see. People are dying without Christ,"[2] Dave Swartz reminds us. This is reality. Whether the people around us acknowledge this truth or not, it is a fact that they need the Lord Jesus Christ. Christians must break down the protective, exclusive barriers they erect and share the good news of the gospel openly with everyone.

I learned a valuable lesson concerning this from Dr. Dennis Hensley of Fort Wayne, Indiana. A freelance writer and author of several books and hundreds of articles, Dennis is a committed Christian. He writes and speaks frequently to both Christian and secular audiences.

He is entertaining, interesting, well informed, and uncompromising in his Christian faith. When he speaks, he simply integrates his faith into his speech, choosing his subject and words in the same manner as if he were speaking to a room full of Christians. No one leaves without realizing that he is a Christian, yet no preaching has occurred.

Although he avoids Christian jargon, he speaks of God's work in his life matter-of-factly. He's comfortable with being a Christian. Are you?

In *Think like Jesus,* George Barna writes, "Ninety-one percent of all born-again adults do not have a biblical worldview; 98 percent of all born-again teenagers do not have a biblical worldview. . . . Let's put this in perspective. As of 2003, the United States has about 210 million adults. About 175 million of them claim to be Christian. About 80 million are born-again Christians. Roughly 7 million have a biblical worldview. This is just one out of every 30 adults in this nation."[3]

What is a biblical worldview? It's an understanding and knowledge of the Bible that is sufficient to enable us to evaluate the circumstances and realities of life in light of the Bible's truth. It equips us to make life decisions that are consistent with biblical truth. Do you know the Bible that well? That's the first place to start as you seek to communicate your faith to the world. Spend enough time in God's Word daily so that it can be the grid by which you evaluate every situation and the foundation on which you speak to those around you.

What else hinders us from speaking about our faith? Most of us struggle with a desire to please others. We want to be accepted and loved. Often fear of the opinions of others stifles our witness for Jesus. Paul told us in Galatians 1:10: "Am I now trying to win the approval of men, or of God? Or am I trying to please men? If I were still trying to please men, I would not be a servant of Christ."

Before his heavenly departure, Christ's commission to us was: "Go into all the world and preach the good news to all creation" (Mark 16:15). For some of us, maybe the fullest implications of the good news seem too difficult to condense into a brief conversation.

Clarify the Message

Perhaps we are vague about the message we are trying to communicate. Simply put, the good news is this:

- All men are infected with the deadly virus: sin. Paul wrote, "All have sinned and fall short of the glory of God" (Rom. 3:23).
- God in his holiness cannot tolerate or even look upon sin; so no sinful man can experience communion with him apart from Christ.
- Sin carries the penalty of death. "The wages of sin is death" (Rom. 6:23).
- God sent Jesus Christ to live a perfect, sinless life. Since we are all sinners and unable to live that perfect life, Jesus died to pay the penalty for our sins. He arose from the dead so that we who believe in Jesus Christ can be alive to God again. We can experience both his communion now and eternally in heaven (John 14:15–19).

The ramifications of salvation are expansive, but these basic truths enable us to define the good news of Jesus Christ's life, death, and resurrection. No one is complete without a relation-ship with God. That relationship comes through belief in Jesus, his work, his death, and his resurrection. Only through this is a relationship with God possible.

Be Willing to Drop Kernels of Truth

Now that we understand the good news we want to com-municate, how can we share these truths in the limited time we spend with others? Remember that you don't have to say it all.

Mark Littleton writes in his article, "Plant Seeds, Not Burning Bushes": "What can you do when you wish to share Christ with others in the midst of our fast-paced world that barely has time to taste food, let alone truth? There's a tendency we feel that we need to present the 'whole gospel.'"[4] He points out that the Bible is full of short conversations and messages.

Just as the sower threw out the seed in the parable Jesus told (Luke 8:5–15), God will equip us to share a kernel of truth with those around us. He can later use this small effort to produce a rich harvest. Our responsibility is to willingly speak of our faith in Jesus and the impact he has had in our lives. It is then the Holy Spirit's ministry that accomplishes God's work of redemption.

These past few years I've felt freer to talk about Christ. Why? I've realized it isn't my responsibility to convert but to communicate. Wherever we are each day, there are opportuni-ties for a few words which may plant a seed of hunger and desire in the heart of a nonbeliever.

Littleton concludes in his article, "A discussion on abortion, business practices, marriage or anything else can be related to scriptural truth if one knows the Bible and can pinpoint an appropriate verse. You don't even have to speak for more than a few seconds."[5]

Reporting in her article "Evangelism on the Job," Anna Marie Larkins quoted Susan Sneed of Denver, Colorado, as saying, "Everyone else is opinionated and convinced about their philosophy of life. Why should a Christian hesitate? People are curious to know someone who has a relationship with the living God."[6]

Overcome Fear

What about fear? I know few people who can honestly say they have no fear of witnessing. Since we are human and often self-centered, we not only fear rejection by others, but we fear their ridicule. What will they say if I mention Jesus Christ? We often fail to think of the humiliation, rejection, and shame Jesus experienced for us. But we shouldn't forget his words, "If anyone is ashamed of me and my words in this adulterous and sinful generation, the Son of Man will be ashamed of him when he comes in his Father's glory with the holy angels" (Mark 8:38).

Glenn Plate writes: "Let's face it: Fear will not go away. It must be overcome. I have shared my faith a thousand times, but to this day, I have a 'fear attack' every time I begin. . . . Our fear of witnessing to co-workers and others comes when we focus on ourselves. But God's power enables us to focus on the lost. Perspective changes fear. This speeds us on our way toward the activity of evangelism."[7]

Dave Swartz adds, "We really have something to talk about in Christ. We don't need to be intimidated. God wants our availability far more than he cares about sophistication or experience."[8]

A spontaneous witness to someone in a brief setting has great value in providing opportunities for evangelism. The combination of genuine caring mixed with the verbal expression of our faith leads to effective evangelism. Church statistics indicate that the largest number of people begin attending a church and often come to Christ through an invitation from a friend or family member who has taken time to build a relationship with them.

Boyd Nixon, vice president of Wells Capitol, Inc. in Norcross, Georgia, said that he'd learned several things about witnessing through experience. "One is to be willing to spend years building a relationship. Another is that God engineers circumstances to create significant needs in which his love can be demonstrated. A third is that to show God's love, all I really have to do is listen to someone who needs to talk and needs to know that someone cares."

Identifying interests, needs, and concerns in a person's life and taking time to develop a closeness with them opens a door to your own life, character, and deeds. On hearing your words of faith in the God you love, the listener can see the impact Christ has had on your life, adding credibility to your message of God's faithfulness. "If our role is merciful friendship toward hurting people," writes Pete Hammond, "rather than gospel verbosity, we can relax. We're not in charge, God is."[9]

He further suggests that by following Jesus' example, we can communicate our desire to help each person by discovering what's needed—a testimony of grace; biblical information about the cross, sin, and repentance; or a quiet deed of mercy. Whatever we do, our obedience can open salvation's door for a lost and hurting world.

Begin with Prayer

Where do we begin? Prayer is our starting point. We are simply willing instruments, but he alone knows the heart of the other person, their experiences, circumstances, and needs. We must depend on him to guide the people to us whom we are to meet. He will provide the opportunities.

Bill Bright offers this suggestion: "When you wake up each morning, thank the Lord that He lives within you and ask Him to use your lips to speak of His love and forgiveness at every opportunity throughout the day. . . . Pray and expect God to enable you to introduce His Son into the conversation."[10]

We can take our prayer life to the marketplace, according to Dave Swartz. He says that anywhere we find people—in malls, restaurants, neighborhoods, or at work—we can pray for them on the spot. In her article "Guaranteed to Bloom," Bonnie Bruno adds, "How much easier it is to prepare through prayer, plant in trust and then leave the outcome to God."[11]

What are ways you can be a leader in encouraging and equipping other women to evangelize? Are there innovative programs you can begin in your church that provide outreach to your community? These are some of the questions you may be grappling with.

Use These Ideas for Beginning a Personal Evangelism Ministry

Creative evangelistic tools are limitless, based on your situation and your sensitivity to the Holy Spirit's guidance. Many individuals and groups have developed effective outreach opportunities. Here are a few that you may use for personal evangelism.

- When walking, drop by a neighbor's home to compliment her on her garden. Invite her to coffee or chat, and follow up by taking cuttings, bulbs, or a gardening book to her at a later date.
- Invite a single parent for coffee, lunch, or dinner.
- Welcome a new neighbor with an offer to help her move, a loaf of fresh-baked bread, or an hour of babysitting.
- Visit a woman to pray and talk.
- Invite neighborhood children for a cookie-baking party during Christmas or Easter holidays.
- Write a letter to a college student and possibly include a Christian tract.
- Volunteer for PTA projects, schoolroom mother responsibilities, Scout leadership, coaching an athletic team, or community club activities such as Optimist or Rotary. These are excellent places to build credibility and relationships for future witness.
- Arrive early at work to pray for each coworker, asking God for opportunities to share your faith.

- During lunch ask a fellow worker, "How would you like me to pray for you?"
- Distribute cards to friends and coworkers saying, "If you're ever in need of prayer or know of someone else who needs prayer, call me. My phone number is . . ."
- Become the welcomer in your community, greeting new families with a basket of goodies and a map of the community that shows the most popular stores, malls, and recreation spots. Include a church bulletin or brochure and a personal invitation to visit your church.
- Adopt a single-parent family or a lonely foreign-exchange student.
- Write a letter for the Letters to the Editor column of your local newspaper about issues important to Christians.
- Send an anonymous subscription to a Christian newspaper or magazine to an unchurched family or individual.

A person could begin an evangelistic outreach similar to the one described in the article "Sharing 9 to 5." Glenn Plate says:

> We moved to San Diego in September 1980. We didn't know anyone in the city. For three months, my wife and a friend clipped names out of the social section of newspapers and magazines. We added to the list the names of people I had befriended on the job. By December we had seven hundred names. Then, to create an environment in which to help reach these people for Christ, we planned an evangelistic dinner party. We mailed

seven hundred engraved invitations to people we didn't know. The night of the event, fifty people showed up at a downtown hotel. Seventeen indicated that they prayed and received Christ that night.[12]

They continue to hold three evangelistic parties each year, hosting from 175 to 200. They've seen 250 people become participants in Bible study groups and have started a denominational church with 300 in attendance each week. Not all of us can follow Glenn Plate's example, but there are many other evangelistic ministries that begin in the home.

Gladys Hunt describes one of these in her *"How-to" Handbook for Inductive Bible Study Leaders*. She writes, "In the area of initiating a Bible study, the first hurdle is inviting someone to study the Scripture with you. That can be a scary idea. What if you're turned down? Pray for one contact, one good conversation that can lead into spiritual things. Ask God to open your eyes to see people who are really eager to know what the Bible says."[13]

One of my friends has a fall coffee each year where she invites neighbors for a casual time of getting acquainted. After refreshments she gives a sheet asking them to list their interests, favorite hobbies, and so forth. She then asks if they would like to meet weekly or monthly with others of similar interests.

Another question asked was, "Would you be interested in a Bible study with other neighbors on a weekly basis?" Invariably she receives enough *yes* answers to the last question to begin a neighborhood Bible study.

One key to a successful neighborhood Bible study is the use of basic study materials. Once you have decided on study materials, these tips may help in planning your meeting. After a brief time for coffee or refreshments, start the discussion by reading the questions in the guide. Wait for women to share their answers. Keep the numbers small in these groups. This helps people open up and ask questions without embarrassment.

Be a discussion leader, not a lecturer. Facilitate and direct the discussion, but be careful not to dominate. Let the women experience the joy of personal discovery. Finally, close the study with a note of encouragement for the discoveries the women have made and in anticipation of God's insights from his Word for the coming days.

If you are seeking to equip women for the ministry of evangelism, why not invite Christian women for a weekly Bible study in your home? You could use the same basic format as discussed. Encourage them to repeat the study in their neighborhood each week, thus multiplying the number of women involved in Bible study.

Another effective type of evangelism in a neighborhood can center around coffee talks. At these meetings neighbors are invited for a morning get-together with a brief talk by an inspirational speaker. This type of meeting is usually well received if the speaker is known in the community or if it is a holiday event. Be sure babysitting is available to mothers, making it easy for them to attend.

Rebecca Brauhn of Tacoma, Washington, writes and offers another suggestion. She plans a formal Christmas luncheon. Friends, neighbors, and coworkers are invited to a beautiful setting to hear the gospel, starting with the explanation of why we celebrate the holiday. A visit like this can also lead to a weekly neighborhood Bible study.

Pat Cartrelle of Clinton, Mississippi, describes a summertime weekly Bible study held at a friend's house. "Babysitters were with the children in the backyard. We brought a sack lunch and ate together after the Bible study. It was a nonthreatening event for non-Christians."

Remember that God can always use the special talents and gifts he has given in new ways. Pray for creative ideas and suggestions so that you can reach out to others. Identify the gifts that you have.

Are you gifted with children? Provide child care in your home one morning each week during the summer so that mothers can have a day out. Plan crafts, games, and activities centered around a truth in a Bible story that you can read to the children.

Are you a gifted cook or artist? Plan six weeks of cooking or art for interested neighborhood women. I know one woman who has a six-week fall class on holiday baking. Women from the community sign a waiting list to attend. Her faith is integrated into her discussion of Christmas preparations.

Another friend who is an outstanding artist teaches watercolor classes in her home as the vehicle for sharing her faith with strangers and unbelievers. She also offers to speak about her art in local public schools. This, too, gives her an opportunity to witness. Yet another friend teaches an eight-week cooking class each year to the students in her son's elementary class. She has had many opportunities to build relationships with young children and their parents. Through these she has been able to witness outside the classroom setting.

You have the potential to be an initiating force in your church for community outreach. As with any ministry, it begins with prayer. The following situation is an instance in which I was personally involved.

Community Bible Study

One warm June morning a group of friends and I met to discuss a desire we had in common. My husband had just come to pastor a church in the community. He and I were praying for God's clear direction for ministry. My friends Jan and Bonnie began the discussion. "We have a desire to begin a weekly Bible study for the community in our church," Bonnie said. "We started one last year in conjunction with a national Bible study program, but the weekly study lessons were so demanding that many of the women dropped out."

"Yes," Jan agreed, "I have two preschoolers to take care of. Finding a quiet time without distractions is hard enough without trying to spend an hour in word studies every day."

I understand. I had been involved in a similar weekly women's Bible study that I found helpful, but the prerequisites for starting a chapter were extremely limiting.

"I've always felt that a community Bible study has a tremendous outreach potential for the local church," I said. "Why don't we pray and ask God if he'd have us begin our own? I'm willing to write the weekly study sheets if this is God's will. If there's no one else available, I'll even teach a brief lesson.

Let's just begin by praying. If it's God's will, he'll bring it to pass. Otherwise, we can look for other ways to minister."

That's exactly what we did—pray. As days passed, we heard of more young women looking for a weekly Bible study close to their homes, particularly one where the questions included Bible study and inductive personal application. They also wanted a program for their children.

In July we held another meeting for prayer and feedback, inviting several other women who had shown interest. They listened to our plans with excitement and anticipation. God confirmed our desire in prayer, and we felt his go-ahead to begin final planning. The promise we kept before us as we prepared was, "I will give them a heart to know me" (Jer. 24:7).

I accepted the responsibility of coordinating the effort with the help of the others. I developed the following guidelines for our women's Bible fellowship. This program can be used in any local church with church support and a core group of interested women.

Women's Bible Fellowship

Purpose

Bible study goals are to provide a teaching based on biblical passages with a focus on topics relevant to women or studies of specific Bible books. There will be two sessions each year—a fall session of approximately thirteen weeks, lasting from mid-September through early December, and a spring session from mid-January through early May of approximately sixteen weeks.

Nursery and Children's Program

Nursery will be provided for all participants. A children's program will be developed for children ages two through five years.

Ministry Responsibilities

Discussion group leader—The responsibilities of the discussion group leader are:

• To guide the group's discussion to discover the truth being conveyed.

• To encourage the women, not lecture or counsel.

• To view the women as placed in the group by God.

• To pray for each of the women in the group on a regular basis. Let them know you're praying for them. Encourage them in their prayer life.

• To take time to talk with anyone who doesn't know the Lord and build a friendship, giving opportunity for future witness.

• To study the Word daily.

• To help the women establish a consistent habit of Bible study, encouraging the women to complete the daily portion of their study sheet, helping them find a good time to study, and phoning them during the week, if possible.

• To initiate monthly luncheons.

• To introduce the prayer ministry at the second luncheon of each study. Members agree to *pray* for the personal prayer requests of other small-group members daily. Confidentiality is a prerequisite. One person is selected to record answers to prayer, and these are shared at luncheons.

Lecturer/teacher—The responsibilities of the lecturer/ teacher are:

• To present a weekly lecture that accurately summarizes biblical content of the lesson. The leader should give careful attention to the application of the content to a woman's life. The Scripture states that a teacher of biblical truth is held accountable by God for her teaching. Therefore, the lecturer should schedule enough time for conscientious study of the material to be presented.

• To prepare the opening time by either leading it or asking others to do so. In this time each week, a brief devotional, insightful teaching concerning the day's lesson or special music is presented to introduce the day's study before everyone breaks into small groups for the discussion time.

• To meet with the discussion leaders and children's coordinators on a regular basis or as often as necessary to ensure a smoothly run Bible study.

• To help in the selection of the following year's leadership team—discussion group leaders, children's teachers, and nursery workers.

• To help plan the following year's study.

Discussion Group Procedures

I. Preparation for discussion (by discussion leaders)

   A. The room

      1. Have room set up ahead of time.

      2. Make a name tag for each woman to wear throughout the year.

   B. First day

      1. Let each woman introduce herself.

      2. Start question-and-answer period with women. Hearing another woman participate helps others who may be more reticent.

      3. Be relaxed. Make everyone feel welcome.

      4. Inform the women that any Bible translation is acceptable. Point out, however, that different wording among translations might make a difference in answers.

II. Leading discussion

   A. How to encourage participation

      1. Verbally create a relaxed atmosphere.

      2. Introduce new women to the rest of the group.

      3. Select an enthusiastic person to start the lesson.

      4. Keep all discussions centered around study questions. If someone asks an unrelated question, save it for a luncheon or to discuss privately.

      5. Encourage volunteering.

      6. If no one answers a question, call on different women by name. Do not be afraid of brief periods of silence. Wait for a volunteer before calling on someone.

7. Occasionally ask, "Can we hear from someone who hasn't answered a question yet?"

8. Avoid tangents. Be bold and guide the discussion to the relevant question.

9. Avoid irrelevant questions. Say, "Can we talk about this at another time?" Don't even try to answer.

10. Encourage women to finish their lesson each week, studying on a daily basis.

11. Question the entire group for their thoughts when asked what you (leader) think. If there is no comment, a leader's response is acceptable.

12. Go to the next question if no one shares an answer to a question.

13. The leader can share at times on questions marked "personal."

14. It is preferable to stay in the Scripture passage under study when discussing any question in or related to those on the study sheets.

B. How to handle wrong answers

1. Suggested responses might be:

a. Are there other thoughts about the question?

b. I'd be interested in knowing what some of the others have discovered.

c. Could we have some more sharing on this?

2. Clear-cut wrong answers.

a. Allow other members to give additional input. If a correct answer is brought out, the leader should summarize and move on.

b. If the error continues, turn to the Scripture passage, read it again, and, as the leader, summarize the passage.

3. Partial truth.

a. Ask for more insights and try to draw out the correct answer.

b. State the answer sought and why.

4. Salvation question.

a. If their answer about personal salvation is wrong, ask, "What does the Bible say about it?" And show them other Scriptures.

b. If it comes up but is not a question in the lesson, recognize this an opportunity to talk privately with that person later. Give an encouraging answer in the group session. As soon as the session concludes, ask the person if she can stay to talk or schedule a conversation within a few days.

Luncheons

Monthly luncheons are regularly scheduled. They are informal to prevent competition. No husbands or children are invited. Extended nursery should be provided on that day. Keep conversation edifying. Occasionally invite the teacher/lecturer to join you.

Setting Up Luncheons

Discussion leader announces luncheon at regular meeting. She gives date, helps decide on type of luncheon, and asks for a volunteer hostess. (Hostesses provide beverage while another member brings dessert.)

The hostess distributes a sign-up sheet with the needed food contributions marked or tells what each woman can bring. Extended care is provided by the church. Only nursing infants should attend luncheons. Discussion leader writes thank-you note to the hostess.

Types of Luncheons

Sack lunch—Each person brings a sandwich and a piece of fruit. Sandwiches are quartered and placed on a platter. All fruit is combined for fruit salad. Everyone in the small group shares.

Salad luncheon—Each woman brings her favorite salad.

Large tossed salad—Each woman brings an assigned ingredient, and then all are tossed together for a shared salad.

Taco luncheon—Each woman brings a designated ingredient for tacos which are assembled at the luncheon.

Overstuffed-potato luncheon—Each member is asked to bring one ingredient (sour cream, chives, broccoli, cheese, and so forth) for overstuffed potatoes.

Hero sandwich—Each woman brings either a meat, cheese, vegetable, or loaf of French bread to be combined.

International or one-country luncheon—Each woman brings her favorite foreign dish or a dish related to a designated country.

Luncheon Discussion

• Questions brought up in discussion-group time that can be handled at a luncheon are a possibility. (No lengthy discussion or research questions pertaining to lesson.)

• Ideas from lessons such as "joy" could be used to let women share opportunities they have had to be a joyous servant.

• Ways of modeling a life of prayer for our children.

• Holiday topics could be considered each month. For example, in February, each one can share her favorite Scripture verse on love or a recent act of love she received.

• Tell about the person who has had the greatest influence on your spiritual life.

• Tell about one childhood memory that reflects God working in your life since birth.

In order for many women to participate, a children's program coordinator will need to be enlisted to care for children while their mothers attend the Bible study. The following suggestions come from Bonnie Cook, Weaverville, North Carolina.

• A program including Bible study, crafts, and games will be formed for children ages three through five. Available curriculum material will be evaluated and selected by those in leadership with women's Bible fellowship.

- Before September contact children's workers by mail or phone. The workers will be paid weekly for their involvement. Mothers who attend the Bible study will assist as necessary on a volunteer rotation system.
- Submit to the church treasurer estimated cost for monthly nursery and children's program expenses.
- Photocopy any color pictures and prepare visual aids and craft supplies prior to each week's meeting.
- Arrive one-half hour before children and arrange chairs, toys, and so forth. Make certain cups, napkins, and juice are available.
- During monthly luncheon meetings, have necessary nursery workers available for mothers and set time for mothers to return from the luncheon.

I prayerfully asked different women if they would serve as discussion leaders. An advertisement was designed and posted on bulletin boards and grocery store windows throughout the town. We decided on a convenient time schedule and selected the rooms for the discussion groups to meet. The lecture and opening time were held in the church chapel. A leadership training meeting was scheduled for a morning prior to the first official Bible study.

On the first day women arrived and registered after hearing of the study through neighbors, radio spots, and newspaper articles. In the opening session leaders were introduced, the program was explained, and an introduction to the book to be studied was given. After that, the first study sheet was distributed followed by a period of fellowship and refreshments.

The next week the leaders divided the women into small groups and made name tags. We decided to use the following time schedule:

9:45–10:15 a.m.	Discussion leaders have prayer meeting
10:15–10:30 a.m.	Opening time in the chapel
10:30–11:20 a.m.	Small-group discussion time
11:20–12:00 p.m.	Music and lecture in chapel

In one year our study has grown from the original twenty-five to eighty registrants. We thank the Lord for all the lives he has touched through this ministry.

By your prayerful use of some of these suggestions, God will show you creative ways in which you can have an evangelistic ministry. In the next chapter we will talk about how you can take some of these same ideas to develop a churchwide program that will become a vital outreach in your community and the world.

Chapter 7

WOMEN REACHING THE POOR IN CHRIST'S NAME

"WITH THE EVER-INCREASING TREND toward urbanization, cities are offering opportunities for evangelization–simply because that's where the people are,"[1] writes William J. Brown. He mentions that the urban population increases at a yearly rate of 3 percent, twice as fast as that of the world's population.

In 2000, 55 percent of the world lived in cities, and by the year 2050, this figure will increase to 80 percent according to Brown. In 1900, there were only twenty world-class cities with over one million people that were considered international. It is thought that by 2050 there may be as many as nine hundred such cities.

Is it your desire to see your city, community, town, or valley reached for Jesus Christ? We all know that with God nothing is impossible. If you have a desire to reach the poor in your city, is it founded in him and completely dependent upon him? If so, then the possibilities are staggering.

Who are the poor in your community? Jesus tells us in Matthew 5:3, "Blessed are the poor in spirit." The poor in spirit include anyone who admits to a spiritual bankruptcy, those who are searching for answers and meaning in life.

You have the potential to be an initiating force in your church for community outreach. As with any ministry, it begins with prayer. Ideas for community evangelism are suggested in this chapter. Prayerfully consider whether God is leading you to implement one of these in your community.

There are many ways you can reach out to your community. Advertising is a method being used by both church growth teams and new churches.

Community Advertising

Have you considered preparing advertisements for your church? Design a few ads and show them to your pastor and church leaders. Dewey Davidson, pastor of the Park Street Baptist Church of Greenville, Texas, says, "I want to reach the 'common Joe' who doesn't think much about Christ and won't let you in the house to talk to him. I can reach this kind of person through the newspaper. My ads are down to earth—where people are."[2]

Pastor Wally Hostetter of the Faith Evangelical Church of Rochester, Michigan, praises the benefits of advertising by saying, "Faith took aim at the target by first doing a survey in the community without mentioning the church name. The results became the basis for the program."

Hostetter explains: "We found that the number one reason people don't go to church is because of boring sermons that don't relate to life. The second reason was the perception that all the church wants is money. The third reason was that church members are seen as 'holier than thou' and hypocrites. We believed it was our call to address each of these issues and offer ministries to benefit the individual. The church began an aggressive ad campaign, advertising in seven community newspapers. Titles like 'Holier Than Thou We're Not,' 'Spend Easter in a Gym' (their current meeting place), and 'He Won't Make You Yawn' sprang from the pages to grab attention."

The well-written spots avoid any Christian catchwords; they simply focus on Faith's friendliness, the interesting and practical sermons, and the church's emphasis on the person, not his money.

Besides newspaper ads, direct mailing and radio spots have been added which helped to increase their church membership from 19 to 470 at Easter four years later. Looking for a new approach to reach the unchurched? Try advertising. It works.

Summertime Ministries

Vacation Bible School has the potential for vibrant outreach. Too often we become entrenched in old methods resulting in a lifeless program. Attendance drops, and the real opportunity for community outreach is abandoned.

A Midlothian, Virginia church member saw this happening in her church. Disinterest was the norm for the regular June Vacation Bible School. Volunteers were scarce, and enthusiasm was at low ebb. An elementary schoolteacher, she decided to develop a program with variety and activities to excite any child.

First, she startled the congregation by abandoning the traditional June date and announcing that the program would be delayed until the first week of August. Convinced that children dread the thought of another "school" immediately after the beginning of summer vacation, she scheduled August as a time when the excitement of vacation had waned.

She also changed the typical VBS format. Knowing from years of teaching experience that children need movement, variety, and a change of scenery, she developed a program where the children would not meet with the same teacher for the Bible story, crafts, music, and games in the same location. Children would move about during the day.

By using the special talents of the individual teachers, she felt an exciting alternative to the traditional Vacation Bible School could be developed. Her new program was so successful it proved to reach out to several unchurched families. The following format was used:

Vacation Bible School (VBS)

9:00–9:15 a.m.   Morning exercises—can be held as an entire group or in individual classrooms.

Ages 3–5	Grades 1–2	Grades 3–4	Grades 5–6
Gathering Place			
11:00–11:20	9:15–9:35	10:25–10:45	9:50–10:10
Snack			
9:55–10:05	9:40–9:50	10:50–11:00	10:15–10:25
Music			
9:15–9:30	10:00–10:15	9:40–9:55	10:30–10:45

Children met in classrooms at all times. Teachers were encouraged to plan some outside activities, if possible, during classroom time.

Classroom Activities

1. Bible lesson
2. Simple related craft activities
3. Bible-verse memorization
4. Talks by visiting missionaries, pastors, and so forth. (Once a retired minister assumed the role of Daniel and visited the third-grade classroom.)
5. Skits or activities related to theme

Music

1. Relate music to Bible study. Keep it simple.
2. Make or borrow rhythm instruments for younger children.

Gathering Place

Use several interest centers. The teachers assign each child to an interest center each day so that they have an opportunity to visit a different one during the week or day. Usually a child can visit the audiovisual center and one other center in one day.

Audiovisual center—Use films, filmstrips, puppets, and so forth.

Craft center—Make something to share with others such as a mural, items for nursing home patients, bookmarks, scrapbooks, and so forth.

Reading/game center—Include Bible books, storybooks, and Bible games. (A teacher can read a story to the younger children.)

Duties of Director

1. Seeks volunteers and arranges for bulletin announcements.

2. Assigns duties to volunteers according to their strengths and experience.

3. Arranges workshop so that all Vacation Bible School teachers are familiar with material being used. Each should know *what* to do and *how* to implement it. The teacher should construct each craft project before it's introduced to the children. A completed sample is always helpful.

4. Publicizes Vacation Bible School; encourages congregation to contact friends and neighbors; oversees the designing of posters; and prepares notices for parents, teachers, and so forth.

5. Substitutes for absent teachers.

6. Maintains records of attendance and procures food and supplies.

Time Schedule

March—Select committee to review and select VBS material. Order review copies to consider. Make selection and place order.

May—Announce dates of VBS to congregation. This will give parents time to consider family vacation time. Include questionnaire in Sunday bulletin with registration form to be completed. Include space for volunteers to sign up. Collect craft booklets, teachers's guides, and so forth to use for teacher training sessions.

June—Schedule teacher training sessions.

July—Purchase craft supplies, design posters, place ads in newspapers, and so forth. Make a large banner for the church-yard. Set up rooms in preparation for August VBS. Meet with teachers to see if there are any last-minute changes or preparations. Explain class movements to gathering place, music, and snack areas. Give children's names and class assignment lists to teachers.

The night of the last day of VBS, a program is presented so that parents can see their children's work, enjoy the music, and observe the things they have learned. The music director, working with the other teachers, plans the program. Notices of the program should be sent to parents one or two days before. (The daily activities should not be geared to this program. It should be the outgrowth of the week and a summation of lessons learned about God and the Bible.)

Summertime family workshops can be used as an outreach tool. Two-week nighttime programs for all family members can be developed to include friends and neighbors of church members. Each meeting could be self-contained, even if a central theme is used. With this visitors can come for as many evenings as they wish and still benefit. Each program could begin with a family outing or meal before dividing the participants by age groups into small-group Bible studies, discussions, or activities.

Other summer ministries might include Backyard Bible School, neighborhood Bible clubs, or day camp. The Westminster Church of Greenville, Texas, conducted a Backyard Bible School one summer behind members' homes. Children living in the neighborhood walked from house to house in different areas of the Bible schools and invited neighbors to join in the music, crafts, games, Bible story, and refreshments. The children involved in this felt adventurous, which added to the appeal.

Community Women's Outreach Ministries

A number of other successful community outreach ministries can be initiated that minister to the needs of women. In MOPS, the Mothers of Preschoolers program, mothers meet for an informal lunch and craft program, ending with the personal testimony of a Christian woman.

Cathy Culbertson writes that MOPS meets the needs of "one of the most isolated stressed-out groups of women in America." For more information about this program, contact MOPS, Focus on the Family, Colorado Springs, Colorado 80995.

Mothers' Morning Out is another successful neighborhood program. Through this ministry a church provides babysitting services one morning a week for mothers of small children, giving them three free hours.

Carol King of Mt. Holly, North Carolina, writes, "'Mothers' Morning Out' gave us the opportunity to meet women in the neighborhood, serve them and establish friendships, and then invite them to church. We had a paid employee/coordinator and one church mother assistant each week. The mother was charged one dollar per child for the entire morning. The child could bring a lunch, if he wished."

Moms in Touch is an organization for mothers who meet to pray for their public-school children. The purpose statement of the organization is "to intercede for children through prayer and to pray that our schools may be guided by biblical values and high moral standards." For more information, write Moms in Touch, c/o Fern Nichols, 14636 Poway Mesa Dr., Poway, California 92064-2960.

Craft Get-together is another evangelistic program, which offers women with common interests the opportunity to meet in a nonthreatening environment to hear the gospel. Women in the community who enjoy crafts meet once a week to learn a new craft technique or develop an old one while enjoying the fellowship of Christian women.

After the craft segment of the meeting, a Bible study follows with discussion. One woman describes this as a "neighborhood outreach in small groups combining common interests (such as exercise, cooking, sewing, or crafts) with evangelism in a friend-ship setting."

One church rented a public meeting hall downtown to host their program, drawing many women with handicraft interests who did not normally attend church.

Lunch Break Bible Study is another outstanding women's ministry that several churches have begun. Once a month working women in the community are invited to a prepared lunch at the church. A thirty-minute Bible study is included. It is their responsibility as Christian women to minister to the many working women who have limited time and opportunities for fellowship.

Ministries for Children

Besides summertime ministries there are a variety of creative ways to reach neighborhood children for Christ.

Good News Clubs are after-school programs that focus on evangelism and discipleship while children are invited for a time of Bible study, activity, games, and supper. For more information write Child Evangelism Fellowship, Box 348, Warrenton, Missouri 63383.

Awana or Pioneer Clubs are similar to scouting programs with Christian emphasis and projects. Badges are earned, camping trips taken, and skills in many areas explored. The addresses for these organizations are: AWANA Youth Organization, 3215 Algonquin Road, Rolling Meadows, Illinois 60008 and Pioneer Club Ministries, 1800 St. Charles St., Wheaton, Illinois 60189 or Box 47, Burlington, Ontario, Canada L7R 3Y3.

Other children's programs include Crossfire, a program for troubled street children available in the downtown city area of Butler, Pennsylvania. A church in Orangeburg, South Carolina, holds a Back to School party in August for foster children in their community. "Church participants gave children school supplies, bags, lunchboxes, and a Bible," writes Linda Wells.

Another ministry group that women can start is a Latchkey Kids program for children who come home to an empty house. In this weekly program children are offered a place to come or assigned an adult to call when frightened or lonely.

Tips for a Community Ministry

Other program ideas to reach the poor in body and spirit were gathered from a recent survey of church workers:

- Through an area social worker, find out about needs for food or clothing and help meet these needs.
- Contact school principals to discover ways you can help needy children with food and clothing.
- Teach a foreign language to willing church members who wish to evangelize the foreign-speaking population in your town. Start English classes for the foreign-language speaking residents in your city.
- Become involved with the Angel Tree Project, a Prison Fellowship International ministry, providing and delivering Christmas gifts to children of prisoners.
- Start a free community lunch program, serving lunch the last five days of the month to needy families to help them stretch their food budgets.
- Invite international students into your home for meals, family occasions, holidays, or special community events.
- Plan a luncheon honoring an international wife or mother as a welcome by the community, showing an interest in her culture and inviting her to talk about it.

- Find families willing to host unwed mothers in their homes as they await the birth of their children, or provide clothing, furniture, and friendship to a lonely unwed mother.

- Sponsor refugees from foreign nations who need a new start.

- Haven Home and Haven of Rest mission homes for street people provide a much-needed ministry. Helping supply these homes can be a church outreach program. One sixth-grade Philadelphia child sponsored a move to give blankets to the homeless that became a successful community-wide ministry.

- Homes for battered women and children often need supplies and food. Women in the First Presbyterian Church of Daytona Beach, Florida, joined with other church-women to sponsor an ongoing project of supplying food, paper products, toothpaste and brushes, diapers, and other essentials. Almost every community has a secret refuge for these women, usually represented by a social agency that seeks community help.

- Start a prison visitation or a Bible study program. One pastor takes food each month for a potluck supper in the jail. He and congregational members pray with the inmates, conduct a service, and serve a meal.

- Collect eyeglasses for a Christian medical association to be used for the needy.

- Women Connection, sponsored by several California churchwomen, brings needy community women to church where they are served a light supper and given a simple devotional and program. A church in Daytona Beach, Florida, picks up needy residents of a public nursing home one day each week and drives them to the church for lunch and a brief devotional. The outreach program has been an inspiration to all involved.

- Tutor local teenagers. Build relationships and help struggling schoolchildren.
- Hold classes (beauty, sewing, fashion, high school equivalency, and so forth) for women in prison to prepare them for a useful life upon their return to society.
- Start a circulating library of Christian books for a nursing home and hospital patients.
- Make baby clothes and send them to a crisis pregnancy or child abuse center.
- Offer to teach a Bible study to long-term patients in the hospital. Plan entertainment for the children's ward and donate Christian books for the book cart.

The North Buncombe Samaritan Ministries (NBSM) of Weaverville, North Carolina, sponsors another ministry opportunity. It was developed by a cooperative effort of the local churches to meet the needs of needy travelers. A network was set up to identify those with legitimate needs and to help them as they move to new jobs and opportunities.

NBSM, which is centrally located in the town, is "the outreach of a group of churches that tries to make the love of God revealed in Jesus Christ real to people in need," Jo Osborne, an area participant, explains. She says, "The ministry is equipped to assist in financial emergencies (rent, oil, gas, electricity, medicine, and lodging), as well as providing food."

The ministry has developed a statement of policies, boundaries, and procedures for volunteers and ministers who serve in the office. All the clients are entered into a countywide database of social-related organizations. Though the ministry cannot meet every need, it does serve as an emergency center for many. Detailed confidential records are kept. Financial support comes from churches, individuals, businesses, interdenominational organizations, and civic groups.

Their ministry is based on 2 Corinthians 8:14–15, "At the present time your plenty will supply what they need, so that in turn their plenty will supply what you need. Then there will be equality, as it is written: 'He who gathered . . . little did not have too little.'"

Finally, a program that God might lead you to explore is the Employee Assistance Program. Established by more and more businesses and corporations in our nation, the program helps employers identify employee performance problems. It then provides referral services for those in need. Problems with marriage, alcohol, stress, and other problems can be identified by supervisors and professional assistance offered.

Suggesting a program like this in your workplace or beginning one with health professionals in your church might meet the ever-increasing job-related problems that are prevalent in our nation.

This chapter would be incomplete without a focus on the opportunities to reach those living abroad. Support of foreign missions is of utmost importance to Jesus as seen in the Great Commission. You may ask what laypeople can do to help witness to those far away. There are many creative ways to reach across the seas. The primary way is through personal prayer and financial support of missionaries.

Missionaries are real people who, just like us, get lonely, frustrated, and overstressed. They wash dishes three times a day, manage demanding children, need friends, and need encouragement. All this takes place in a strange environment, different from any many have ever experienced.

Unfortunately, we often view them as a faceless group with super abilities and strengths but with few needs. We admire them, but we don't feel empathy for them. This is simply a false perception. Missionaries need our love and encouragement to keep persevering in the different cultures in which they live.

There are many ways to promote missions and minister to these important messengers. Missions conferences are excellent for meeting missionaries and church workers. Why not make your annual missions conference unique? Instead of the traditional speeches and slides, use innovative ideas like the ones given for planning a women's conference.

Include skits, panel discussions, and tip sheets on ways to emphasize missions in the home and in the church. Plan a special women's missions luncheon for the missionary wives and visiting churchwomen. Seek ways to become personally involved in their lives, praying for individual needs and concerns. Find out the foods and simple items they are unable to find in the country where they serve. Make plans to send care packages on a regular basis.

As a church body, there are other ways of promoting a missions emphasis. It has been said, "A church that is not mission minded will soon become a mission field." Start by beginning a Missionary Minutes program in your church. Ask the pastor if someone can give a regularly scheduled five-minute talk about some aspect of missions before the church service. Entertain visiting missionaries. They sacrifice many things to serve your Lord. Show them you're thankful.

Some churches provide a missionary home as a refuge for missionaries on furlough. They are invited to live there for three, six, or twelve months while they are working throughout the area. This provides a stable home for their family while they are in the United States, allowing the children to attend school regularly. Also, the congregation has an opportunity to know and become friends with the family.

In her article "And How Shall They Hear . . . Without a Letter," Patricia Hershey stresses the deep need missionaries have to hear from friends back home.[3] Quoting Proverbs 25:25, "Good news from far away is like cold water to the thirsty" (TLB). She explains that missionary letters need to be encouraging. You can encourage through personal testimony of God's activity in your life. You can show appreciation to the missionaries by calling them your representative in foreign lands. This helps everyone fulfill Jesus' Great Commission.

If you don't know a missionary, write a personal letter, introducing yourself and showing interest in his or her work. "There is a warm and caring feeling conveyed by a handwritten letter," writes Mrs. Hershey.

Along with the letter send newspaper clippings of relevant articles about the country where they serve. Refer to these in your letters. Don't burden the missionary with heavy personal problems or negative church information. Make it your intent to support and build up.

Pat Hershey also adds, "Receiving cards, gift-wrapping paper, and other mementos of a holiday season is a rare treat." Don't forget birthdays and notes to the children. Missionary children can be easily overlooked and feel neglected. Include humor in your letters; a light touch can be refreshing.

Crafts for Missions Day or Christmas in July are two ways women have joined together a day each year to make gifts for missionary families. Ann Hunt, talking about the program in Saint Andrews Church, Irmo, South Carolina, says:

> Several women in our group made beautiful baskets. Then various craft items are completed for Crafts for Missions Day to fill the baskets.
>
> Hand-made cross-stitched bookmarks, Christmas ornaments, angel tree-toppers, small vine wreaths, and cookie mixes with cookie cutters are included in the gifts. We organize the crafts according to the level of difficulty and make sure everyone has something to do.
>
> The results of the day's fellowship are an increase in missions awareness as well as a basketful of lovely gifts to be mailed out in time for Christmas.

Another idea for Christmas packages came from Susan Miller and Rhonda Moody of Columbia, South Carolina. They purchase a padded manila envelope and fill it with specialty items. Then they select a basket for collecting the treats, one that will hold the same amount as the envelope mailer.

They begin collecting early enough to allow proper time for the package to reach the missionary friend. Then they provide church members with a list of suggested treats. Some of the treats include chewing gum, candy, toothpaste, dental floss, raisins, napkins, pudding, and so forth.

Another women's group formed an Alongsiders ministry. Several women in the church volunteer to pray daily for a woman missionary and her family. They correspond with their distant friend, study the country where she serves, send gifts, and adopt her as a family member.

Now that you see the many ways there are to reach out with the gospel of Jesus Christ, don't hesitate to begin your ministry. The options are extensive. Prayerfully ask God to show you the one ministry that he has tailor-made for you, and develop it for his glory!

Remember Jesus' words, "For I was hungry and you gave me something to eat, I was thirsty and you gave me something to drink, I was a stranger and you invited me in, I needed clothes and you clothed me, I was sick and you looked after me, I was in prison and you came to visit me. . . . Whatever you did for one of the least of these brothers of mine, you did for me" (Matt. 25:35–36, 40).

Chapter 8

WOMEN AND MINISTRIES THAT MEET SPECIAL NEEDS

IN A NATIONAL ADVICE COLUMN in the local newspaper, I read, "I have never written to you before, but I think the following might interest you and some of your readers."

The letter writer described the story of a ninety-one-year-old man. She wrote of the man awakening early, showering, shaving, and getting "dressed up" for the day. He skipped his usual walk to the gas station to prepare for a visit with other old-timers. He sat on his front porch watching the road, waiting.

He also missed his usual afternoon nap, waiting instead in anticipation of a visit from at least one of his six children. Two of his daughters were married and lived close by. They hadn't seen him in a long time. *Surely they'd come today,* he thought. At suppertime, his landlady brought him some ice cream and a small cake, but he didn't eat it. He was saving it to eat with them when they came.

Nighttime came, and the old gentleman went to his room to retire. But first he knocked on his landlady's door and said, "Promise to wake me when they come."

"It was his birthday. He was ninety-one," ends the landlady's letter. Nobody came.

Our world and our churches are filled with hurting people with special needs for care and comfort. Though church programs are designed for all those attending to have a vital place in the life of the church, the special needs of so many are often overlooked.

Susan Hunt in her article "Reach Out and Comfort Someone" writes, "Hurting people require enormous energy just to survive. We can be a further drain on their energies through insensitive remarks or neglect, or we can provide an environment of love that makes it easier for them to experience God's comfort."[1]

How often have you done nothing because you didn't know what to do? Whether people are hurting or just have special needs, the body of Christ can, with sensitivity, minister to those in certain situations. In this chapter we will try to identify some of these groups and offer ministry opportunities to meet their needs.

We have already identified and offered ministry options for two of these groups—mothers of preschoolers and working women. We mentioned the ninety-one-year-old man, so we'll first look at ministry to senior citizens.

Ministry to Older Adults

"The graying of America" is a phenomenon well noted by contemporary sociologists and historians. The size of the aging population of the United States is growing every year, leading to more senior adults in America than ever before. This trend will continue for years to come as the baby boomers, born after World War II, age.

However, many people in the United States have obsolete perceptions of older adults, based on stereotypes of the elderly as unhappy, useless people. Because of our nation's great advances in health care, people are living longer and are in better health than anyone could have predicted even twenty years ago.

In the early years of the United States, age was respected. We will no doubt see a return to that image as senior adults continue in leadership roles and contribute to our nation's betterment.

As Christian believers, we know God equates age with the accumulation of knowledge and wisdom. We read in Proverbs 16:31, "Gray hair is a crown of splendor; it is attained by a righteous life." Proverbs 3:1–2 says, "My son, do not forget my teaching, but keep my commands in your heart, for they will prolong your life many years and bring you prosperity." It is pleasing to God when we respect and minister to his faithful servants.

The following list suggests ways to minister to the needs of senior adults:

1. Senior Saints is a group that meets once each month for a special program and luncheon. Sometimes short trips are planned. It's a Wonderful Life and The Joy Ministry are titles of similar programs in Signal Mountain, Tennessee.

2. Senior Singers is a group of older adults who have designed a complete program of skits, readings, and songs to take to other church senior citizen groups.

3. One church has mobilized members to adopt a shut-in or a senior citizen and visit regularly.

4. One church built an entire retirement village on property adjoining the church location. It is called the Total Living Center and provides mini-seminars, outings, and exciting programs for seniors in the area.

5. Tuesday Tours is a program for older men and women. Besides singing and short informal messages from the minister; programs of special concern are planned. Legal and tax advice, flower arranging, makeup sessions for older women; short museum tours; sandwich and soup lunches; low-impact exercise sessions (even for wheelchair participants); question-and-answer discussions; and crafts are a few of the programs available to them.

6. The value of grandparenting skills is stressed in other programs. In a transient society, the need for grandparents to demonstrate Christian values helps provide stability in an unstable world. This is a priceless contribution and has tremendous potential for ministry. Equipping grandparents to do this more effectively is both appreciated and enjoyed.

Adults Caring for Aging Parents

Alice Brawand, counselor for Wycliffe Bible Translators in Duncanville, Texas, says adults involved in the care of aging parents desperately need support and encouragement. Problems specific to this task can become arduous and extremely draining.

A host of questions confront the adult child. Questions such as: Can the parent be left alone? Should a person be hired to live with the parent? What about nursing homes? If the adult is the only caregiver, will added stresses complicate family life and relationships? What is really best for an older parent? Programs that supply answers and instruction coupled with small caregiver groups for discussion and prayer support are invaluable.

Married Couples in Need of Refreshment

A *Family Circle* magazine article highlighted the top ten family problems.[2] These included power struggles, differences in intimacy needs, communication difficulties, substance abuse, and depression and other psychological disorders.

Marriages and families today are under greater pressures than ever before. Traditional family roles sometimes disintegrate as couples search for direction and continuity. In many cases both parents are forced to work to support the family. The typical traditional family no longer exists.

Churches can help stabilize the American family. The following suggestions are ideas provided by a recent survey of 250 Christian women.

1. Churches can consolidate meetings so several committees and programs reaching different age and need groups are functioning simultaneously. This can prevent family members from having to attend church functions every night of the week. Families should be able to remain at home three to four evenings a week and feel free of guilt imposed by expected attendance at church functions.

2. A Moms and Dads Go Play event is an evening once a month in which couples can spend an evening together.

3. Another church planned a Dinner Out program for couples with a special speaker presenting different aspects of marriage and family life.

4. One church formed a Mother's Fellowship ministry for moms. It met monthly, provided child care, had a special presentation/speaker present a topic of interest such as Teaching Your Child about God, Christian Financial Planning, Healthy Eating, Efficient Housekeeping, and similar seminars. Fellowship and refreshments were part of every meeting.

Bonnie Cook mentioned her church's special presentation for pregnant women entitled Spiritual Preparation for Childhood and Motherhood.

5. One church organized several groups for mothers. Some groups were Mothers of Small Children, Mothers of Adolescents, and Mothers After College. These women met as a support group to incorporate Bible study as they shared concerns and needs.

Homeschool Ministry

Increasing numbers of mothers are choosing to teach children in the home. The church needs to support these efforts by providing out-of-home activities. Lunch Bunch was a program begun in DeLand, Florida, for homeschool mothers. Homeschoolers meet for lunch in the park preceded by a visit to the library.

Special programs on Christian nurturing in education are made available to homeschooling moms as well as others who'd like to participate. It is the responsibility of parents to teach biblical truth and its framework for life to their children as described in Deuteronomy 6:4–9. Homeschooling is one way some Christians accomplish this today.

Divorce and Remarriage

As the statistics of divorce and remarriage continue to sky-rocket, even in the Christian community, provisions should be made to minister to these needs. Beyond theological arguments and placing blame, divorcees, like all others, need to be considered with compassion and love.

One popular church-sponsored program called Fresh Start is for divorced individuals seeking to cope with and recover from the experienced trauma. Other ministries have developed to help the blended family survive the difficulties of achieving unity, particularly when children of each parent are involved.

Seminars, panel discussions, problem-solving sessions, and support groups have proven to be most helpful. In the last decade experts have stated that one of every six children in this country lives in a reconstructed or blended family, and if the trend continues, families with stepchildren will outnumber families raising their own children.

The parenting role is just as difficult as the adjusting marriage relationship. Both teeter like a seesaw in an attempt to maintain balance. Christ's body can reach out a caring hand in these situations of need.

Single Parents

Single parenting follows divorce. Shifting the complete responsibility for home management, child-rearing, and bread-winning to one parent can be an overwhelming experience. The simple things of life become tedious, the "daily-ness" of life burdensome.

Loving Christians can be encouragers and support the single parent.

1. Listen, listen, and listen again. The single parent needs a companion or friend to understand his or her dilemma.

2. Be a supporter. Offer to help around the house. Upkeep of a home can seem an impossible task. Take your husband or a church deacon along to complete simple repairs and maintenance.

3. Provide transportation for children. Often children need help moving from one activity to another.

4. Plan events in your home where both singles and couples with children are invited with or without their children. Don't feel obligated to pair a single with another single person.

5. Offer child care on a regular basis so that the parent can have planned quiet time alone or with friends.

6. Form a Saturday morning women's support group.

7. Invite single-parent families to share family get-togethers with you. This can help to provide role models for the children.

Childless Marriages

The ability to have children is something most of us take for granted; however, one couple out of every six discovers that childbearing is not so easy for them due to a fertility problem according to one expert. In the article "Married, No Children," Becky Foster Steel said that pain often accompanies infertility. "Infertility is a private subject," she wrote, "one that few of us are comfortable talking about. Yet the anxiety the infertile couple feels is very real, and the 'under-wraps' nature of the problem often serves to compound their pain. Those who desire children have no tangible loss to mourn; there are few socially acceptable ways for them to vent their emotions of sorrow and frustration."[3]

How can you minister to these sorrowing couples?

Be informed:

- More couples face infertility today than you may realize. Don't joke about the subject.
- Infertility affects *couples.* It is no one's "fault."
- It is not always a permanent or a lifelong condition.
- Causes are often hereditary and rarely due to sexual promiscuity.
- Childless friends could be under great financial strain as they seek extensive medical assistance.

Be sensitive:

- Realize Mother's Day and holiday times can be extremely difficult. "Growing up, many of us fantasized about how we would celebrate holidays with our children and carry on family traditions. But for those who still have no young ones in the home, holiday times can seem hollow, with festivities bringing painful reminders of their frustration."[4]

- Holiday occasions provide opportunity for well-meaning questions such as, When are you going to give us some grandchildren? This can hurt deeply.
- Be a good listener. Refrain from giving advice. Follow cues in the conversation to express your own thoughts.
- Offer to pray, but don't push.
- Remember that the men involved often are hurting, too.
- Don't pity your friend, treating him or her differently from others. He or she may have reached a point of coping and acceptance and may need your care most of all.

As a Christian woman, you may have struggled or are struggling with this difficult issue in your life. You are probably aware of others who share similar problems.

Have you ever thought of asking these women to consider meeting together for prayer support and encouragement? This may be a ministry God has designed for you that otherwise could be overlooked by the church body. We are encouraged in 2 Corinthians 1:3–6, "Praise be to the . . . Father of compassion and the God of all comfort, who comforts us in all our troubles, so that we can comfort those in any trouble with the comfort we ourselves have received from God."

Those Who Grieve

In our churches those who grieve are often unnoticed, even ignored, after the burial of a loved one. Recently a friend lost her child in the fifth month of pregnancy. I was unaware of the grief she experienced. Whether the loss is a child, spouse, parent, or friend, death is painful. The church needs to be prepared to minister to grieving families.

A Virginia church offers a six-week course led by the pastor on the topic of grief. He deals with the often-experienced emotions that accompany grief and provides biblical encouragement and hope for the day-to-day concerns of the grieving individual.

Fran Caffey Sandin in *See You Later, Jeffrey* describes the emotions that surfaced and the eventual healing that took place in her life after the death of her eighteen-month-old child. She offers suggestions to those who desire to reach out to someone who has suffered loss through death in her article, "10 Ways to Say 'I Care!'"

1. Be present, even if you don't know what to say. Give a hug, squeeze a hand, and don't be afraid to cry.

2. Say something positive about the one who died.

3. Sign the register at the funeral home.

4. Send flowers, sympathy cards, or simple memorial gifts.

5. Encourage the grieving by reassuring them of God's love, but refrain from preaching.

6. Take food to the home in disposable containers.

7. Help the family with practical needs.

8. Be a good listener and be patient.

9. Be aware of the survivor's lonely months ahead. Grieving is a long process. It doesn't end a week or two after the burial.

10. Acknowledge grieving children in the family.

11. Share a book that has helped you.[5]

This, too, is an area of need in which Christ's body can

minister as no other can. Extending the compassionate, loving arm of Jesus Christ to those in need is a calling and a blessing.

Widows

Ministry immediately following the loss of a loved one is essential, but the ongoing needs of the surviving spouse, child, or other family member cannot be ignored. God has much to say in his Word about the widow. "For the LORD your God is God of gods and Lord of lords, the great God, mighty and awesome. . . . He defends the cause of the fatherless and the widow" (Deut. 10:17–18).

Isaiah admonished the people, "Seek justice, encourage the oppressed. Defend the cause of the fatherless, plead the case of the widow" (1:17). Finally, Paul admonished Timothy, "But if a widow has children or grandchildren, these should learn first of all to put their religion into practice by caring for their own family and so repaying their parents and grandparents, for this is pleasing to God" (1 Tim. 5:4).

Though children are told to care for their widowed parents today, often this is not possible due to the distances that separate families. It then becomes the responsibility of Christ's body to care for these precious individuals whom God loves and defends. James told us as believers, "Religion that God our Father accepts as pure and faultless is this: to look after orphans and widows in their distress" (James 1:27).

What are ways that we can do this? "As women, we are particularly sensitive to the needs and concerns of widows, but unless we have 'been there' many of us feel inadequate. We don't all need to assume the role of counselor with all the right words, but we can comfort by extending compassionate love,"[6] Susan Hunt writes.

Churches now are discovering more ways to minister to the widow. I have gathered the following suggestions:

1. Special Ladies are the widows of one church who meet monthly to discuss their problems, followed by luncheon fellowship.

2. In another church deacons are given the names of three widows whom they shepherd, to identify their needs and, when called upon, attempt to solve them.

3. New Beginnings is a group of widows and widowers who meet each month for fellowship and a covered-dish supper.

4. The New City Fellowship Church of Chattanooga, Tennessee, has a vibrant widows ministry. Church officers compiled a list of widows, their needs, and their financial problems, if any. Then they are readily available to help supplement their income when unexpected expenses or emergencies occur.

In addition, interested widows meet weekly for Bible study and prayer. Church work crews take care of house repairs, and vans pick up the women for church services.

Also in conjunction with the ideas mentioned above, the New City Fellowship Church has organized the Chattanooga Widows Fellowship. It has an emphasis on inner-city ministry.

Chattanooga widows have begun the Widows Concert of Prayer. The widows who are involved receive a newsletter; prayer update; listing requests and answers; and other materials to assist them in their ministry of intercession.

"When the Chattanooga Widows Ministry prays, great things happen. For a year, a local prison ministry labored with no conversions. Then the widows agreed to pray for the prison ministry for a year. In that year, 120 prisoners were led to Christ. Imagine the impact which will result when widows across the country are united in prayer!" Terry Gyger concluded in a recent article.

Ministry to Special-Interest Groups

What are creative ways to more effectively nurture our children for Jesus Christ? How can we meet their particular needs when we consider the pressures and stresses that flood their lives?

The following programs have proven effective and may be the ministry God desires for your church.

Small Children

1. Plan children's musicals with choreography, props, and direction to make it as professional as possible.

2. Plan a study for children on Understanding Your Parents. Provide ways that they can show love, obedience, and consideration to parents.

3. Familiarize the congregation with the children of the church. In a Florida church each adult volunteer was paired with a child or family of children and asked to pray for them, greet them by name when they meet, and send cards on special days. Their goal was to encourage more people to become involved in nursery work, Sunday school, children's worship programs, and children's activities through love instead of obligation.

Teens

1. Provide weekly meetings in the church such as Wild Wacky Wednesday for all age groups.

2. Divide teens into small groups that meet one evening a week in homes for Bible study and/or fellowship.

3. Decorate T-shirts and/or plan a luau for Super Sunday Night, a summer fellowship program with Bible study, refreshments, swimming.

4. Fabulous Friends is a program to encourage teens to make a commitment to support one another. Support a teen who plays on a ball team, in a band concert, or performs in another way by attending the events. Help them to recognize the power of praying for one another.

College Students

1. Plan a weeknight Bible study for college students and friends. Include an informal time of singing Christian music accompanied by a guitar, Bible study, and sharing prayer requests.

2. Cuddle a Collegian is a program that encourages church members to be aware of the college students in the church who would enjoy a home-cooked meal, invitation to a concert, or involvement with a family activity.

3. Family Ties is a program where a church family adopts a student for the year and invites him or her into their home throughout the year. It's a great way to show the love of Christ in many small ways!

4. Special events can provide a terrific incentive for college students. They could include a special party with a food theme

such as a fondue or taco or lasagna party. An international dinner with appropriate decorations or a candlelight dinner provide other options.

5. Game Night is a program where college students plan a game night for all ages, children through senior adults. This is a wonderful opportunity for church members to get to know one another and invite non-Christian friends and neighbors.

Everyone brings a favorite game and a snack to share. The evening begins with prayer, and then each member begins to play one of the games. Every thirty minutes everyone switches games. As they proceed, they may choose whom they want to play with the first and last games. For the games in between they must choose to sit with someone who is a stranger.

Career Singles

1. Annual Singles Superstar Event is an activity used for evangelistic outreach. Games, sport contests, and a variety of activities are incorporated in this special event. An annual Hawaiian luau is planned by one church.

2. Quarterly get-togethers, including ski parties and cookouts, are used by one church as an evangelistic tool. Bible study is incorporated in each program.

3. Encouragement Partners is a program that pairs singles and married couples in an informal friendship/discipleship relationship.

4. Young Career Singles is a program held in a home once a month. It includes supper, Bible study, and fellowship. In one church it resulted from the ideas and prayers of a few concerned individuals who wanted to reach out to this particular group.

They determined the Bible leader should be especially competent in his/her biblical knowledge in order to challenge the group. Announcements followed in the church bulletins. Printed cards with the time, date, location, and the leader's name were distributed in the singles Sunday school class. It proved to be a great success.

Others Who Have Needs

The remaining support groups, which could be formed, are as numerous as the individual needs of your church membership. Possibilities include:

1. Overeaters—Design a program for those desiring to lose weight.

2. Something Special—Short-term Bible studies for church members, grouped by age.

3. Women's Night Out—A monthly dinner for all women.

4. Deaf Ministries—Planned get-togethers for the deaf and their families. Coral Ridge Deaf Ministries of Fort Lauderdale, Florida, sponsors a luncheon where participants come from all over the county to meet. The Gangway is a monthly evening of games and snacks.

5. The Compassion Corps—Formed by one church to meet emergency needs for meals, transportation, baby-sitting, moving, and domestic chores.

Members of one congregation are asked to make a double recipe of their family meals, place one recipe in a disposable pan, seal it with foil, freeze it, and bring it to the church to keep on hand. The group receives these frozen meals, dates them, and places them in a freezer designated for that purpose. When the next emergency arises, no calling or frantic preparations are necessary.

Has God burdened your heart with the special needs of a particular group within your church? Pray and ask God to show you how he might use you to meet those needs. It is true that when God calls you, he will equip you for the task. Offer yourself to him today to be his instrument of compassion and caring to those around you.

Chapter 9

WOMEN AND FELLOWSHIP GROUPS THAT ENCOURAGE

I sit in my tattered chair from dawn to dusk. Crossing the
room, even with my walker, is so difficult that often
I don't move for hours. Absently, I flick the television on
and off to watch game shows. Many times, usually in the
silence, the loneliness I fight each day wins its battle,
creeps over my soul, and gnarls my stomach with pain.

I reach for my Bible that sits beside me on the end table.
I open it and read Psalm 23. I read it four or five times a
day. Why doesn't the phone ring? Why is there no knock
on my front door? Where are my church friends with
whom I've shared so many wonderful memories? Am
I forgotten? Why don't they call?

FEELINGS OF ISOLATION are prevalent today for women like Clara. Both the young and the old miss the comfort and encouragement that friendships provide. Hurriedness dominates our society. Activities abound, many with little substance. Only limited time is available for the things that really matter—friends, encouragement, comfort, giving, and caring.

The church is often no different. People come and go, exchanging hurried, sincere greetings in the hallways. Nevertheless, today few relationships are nurtured and maintained. Women lingering on the outskirts often desire to be a part but don't know where or how to begin. They need a caring hand extended to draw them inside.

Then there are women like Clara. Disabled, helpless women who simply need the assurance they have worth. They need to feel wanted and valued. They want to be included even though physical impairment hinders active participation.

Communication and caring are vital to the ministry of Christ's body. The New Testament abounds in passages that include the phrase "one another." *Love, honor, be devoted to, live in harmony with, be kind and compassionate to, accept, serve, spur, encourage, forgive,* and *bear with one another* are only a few of the phrases. God challenges us to reach out to those in need. Christ's church members need to feel connected to complete the picture of his church being that of one body.

Mark A. Taylor writes in his article "Why Community?" that *fellowship* means partnership in the New Testament. "Christians are to be involved with one another. This is the mandate implied in the New Testament comparison of the church to a body. The members of the church, like parts of a body, depend on one another."[1]

We may ask how, then, can we help all women in the church feel included, loved, and cared for? One Texas church faced the problem. The members wondered how they could include a diverse group of women including young mothers who were managing busy homes, the isolated, lonely, older women, and women new to the church.

One of the problems was finding a way to infuse the diverse group with a sense of oneness in the women's ministry. How could they incorporate women of differing backgrounds, experiences, and age groups into one program of support and encouragement?

Women particularly burdened with this problem began to meet for prayer and discussion. They searched for God's solutions and soon developed a program that has been successful.

The new format was based on Hebrews 10:24, "And let us consider how we may spur [encourage] one another on toward love and good deeds." The women realized Paul's admonition was twofold.

There was the aspect of encouragement and also service. They organized a program to meet each of these needs by forming care groups and ministry groups.

Briefly, in describing the ministry groups, they concluded that too often women had grown tired of the burden of service. Sometimes ministry became a grudging task rather than a joyful act in response to Christ's love.

Too often women were asked to do tasks they felt unprepared for or simply disliked. As the leaders studied Christ's gifts to his body, they realized women would give much more cheerfully as volunteers in areas where they felt joy and giftedness when they ministered. The ministry groups were developed as follows:

Foreign and home missions ministry—Send cards, letters, gifts to missionaries, visits, and gifts to shut-ins.

Hospitality ministry—Provide refreshments for Bible school, greeters at Sunday morning services, and graduates' breakfast.

Bulletin board ministry—Design creative ways to present the women's ministry to the church, change these monthly, and announce upcoming events.

Programs ministry—Plan quarterly programs and the church-women's spring retreat and banquet.

Fellowship ministry—Help coordinate dinner on the grounds and any new, interesting homecoming activities; help plan the women's banquet (coordinated effort with programs ministry); plan all-day or weekend spiritual retreat for entire church; provide beverages and set-up for monthly family night covered-dish supper; and provide gifts for graduates.

Prayer ministry—Continue already established Prayer Band.

Helps ministry—Organize cleanup after church dinners and family nights and thoroughly clean the kitchen once a month. Coordinate work to be done for church workdays.

Flowers ministry—Provide flowers for the sanctuary each Sunday; decorate for special holidays.

Nursery ministry—Continue already organized program.

Library ministry—Suggest additions to the library and organize the library to make it appealing and accessible to the congregation.

The chairmen of each ministry group were facilitators. It was not necessary for them to personally fulfill all the responsibilities of the group. They coordinated the work through sign-up sheets, phone calls, and other communication methods.

This format was introduced at a special brunch. Women were asked to choose the ministries they were interested in, listing them by first, second, and third choices. They were then divided into small groups. Each woman met with the women who had the same first choice. This core group became a committee. Later, if one ministry lacked enough participants, willing members were asked to switch to their second or third choice.

The committees met once each quarter to plan the next quarter's events. Quarterly luncheons, along with an inspirational speaker, music, and entertainment, were planned. Women who could not otherwise attend the women's activities were invited to attend. A council of elected officers and committee chairwomen from each ministry and care group oversaw the complete program.

Simultaneously support groups called care groups were formed. Every woman who was a member or regularly attended the church was assigned to a care group of from ten to fifteen women. After prayer and consideration, women were selected and asked to serve as coordinators for their group.

Letters were mailed to every woman to explain the program, list the other members of her group and the coordinators. Follow-up calls were made to answer questions that arose.

The purpose of the care groups was to assure that every woman in the church felt part of the women's ministry. Encouragement, prayer, and compassion were the basis for the program. It was desired that the women's ministry move beyond organization to a strengthening fellowship. The hope that women would grow in their relationship with Jesus by experiencing his love was paramount. By reaching out and nurturing the women, the care group leaders and members prayed for a lasting impact.

An important paragraph was inserted in the new format directives. "Care groups are a wonderful way to cause otherwise 'inactive' women to feel cared for and involved. Those who are involved with church ministry and prefer not to attend or are unable to be at the monthly meetings are no longer labeled 'inactive.' They have a place in a care group and are encouraged to attend quarterly inspirational luncheons. The building of relationships is enhanced. Nurturing can take place."

This is just one example of the unity of purpose and the nurturing relationships that can be facilitated by care groups. It can be done in a number of ways. If you are a care group coordinator, you may decide to form a prayer chain among your members. The chain of participating women exchanges prayer requests and answers.

The care-group coordinator can prayerfully develop her own style of ministry, depending on the gifts God has given her. As mentioned, she is a facilitator, an instrument of God's use. She asks him for wisdom and direction.

She may decide to plan a more structured occasion such as a get-acquainted luncheon or weekly Bible study. The direction taken would be determined by the needs and interests expressed by the women.

All women are told that the purpose of caring for one another is the main focus. One member might experience a birth, another a death or illness, or another the loss of a job. As the individual coordinator keeps in touch with each woman, she may discover creative ways that she and other members can minister to this woman.

The coordinator may organize a week of meals with contributions by the other members in the group. A young mother might need babysitting. Another care-group member might need a ride to the doctor's office or grocery store.

How can you start such a ministry? If your church leaders are not ready to form a program like this, think about contacting other women in your geographic area who attend your church. Suggest starting the ministry as a group with the intention of encouraging new members to become known and active in the congregation.

Even if you can't form a care group immediately, there are ways you can become a better encourager. Do you want to express care and concern to those around you?

Encouragement begins first with God. Paul prayed, "May our Lord Jesus Christ himself and God our Father, who loved us and by his grace gave us eternal encouragement and good hope, *encourage* your hearts and strengthen you in every good deed and word" (2 Thess. 2:16, author's italics). So the place to begin is in God's Word so that you can find God's instructions about encouragement.

As God encourages us each day, we learn to reach out and encourage others. It's his desire. To some God bestows encouragement as a special gift. "We have different gifts, according to the grace given us. . . . If it is encouraging, let him encourage" (Rom. 12:6, 8). Yet God commands all of us to be encouragers. "Therefore encourage one another and build each other up, just as in fact you are doing" (1 Thess. 5:11).

Three ways to become an encourager are:

1. Study the people in your life and become sensitive to their needs, interests, and concerns.

2. Give verbal affirmation to others, identifying character qualities or aspects of their life that you admire or appreciate.

3. Develop loyalty that enables you to stand by that person in love even when the warts in his or her life become apparent or when a crisis puts a strain on the relationship.

In a handout, Fran Caffrey Sandin gives several ways to encourage a friend:

1. Write a note of encouragement to someone experiencing difficulty.

2. Prepare a dish for someone who is ill.

3. Be dependable. If you make a promise to pray, teach, or whatever, do it.

4. Join with others in prayer often and in the study of God's Word. Be ready to encourage by telling how God has been faithful in your life. Sharing answered prayer is particularly valuable.

5. Encourage others to exercise their spiritual gifts. Tell them how they have blessed your life.

6. Give a hug to someone who needs it. Being sensitive to God's Holy Spirit will be the key.

7. Encourage others when they do what God has called them to do.

8. Remember that negative criticism wounds the spirit, but positive suggestions tempered with love and understanding can help someone change.

9. Encourage all to go to church where they hear God's Word taught in faith (Heb. 10:25). God is their only lasting

source of help and encouragement. Point people to Jesus, and your work will never be in vain because he alone has the power to act on their behalf.

10. In depression or a time of loss, it's hard to remember God's acts of power that we have experienced. Help others remember God's faithfulness to them in the past.

11. Always be willing to make a telephone call or invite a friend over for a cup of coffee. Time spent with you may be your greatest gift of encouragement if your desire is to show them God's love.

In her article "You Can Be an Encourager," Lucinda Secret McDowell writes, "The most important form of encouragement is the art of listening. Many times just our presence and willingness to listen patiently are needed most. They can assure someone that he or she is not alone in the midst of questions and struggles."[2]

Are you a good listener? You can become a good listener if you follow these tips:

- An active listener listens carefully then paraphrases the speaker's words to be sure that she is clearly understood.
- A good listener is sensitive to the underlying feelings being expressed.
- A good listener shows concern for those feelings and extends compassion.
- A good listener asks questions related to the conversation, not to pry but to show genuine interest in the subject.
- A good listener responds positively and directs the speaker to biblical truth without making comments reflecting a judgmental attitude.

- A good listener retains a spotless reputation for keeping confidences.
- A good listener does not respond, "I know exactly how you feel!" when she doesn't. One can empathize without inferring complete understanding.
- A good listener does not redirect every conversation to herself.
- A good listener does not feel she always has to give the right answer.

Two types of situations can often arise in the ministry of caring. One is the need to minister to someone who is grieving. In chapter 8, we listed ways to comfort them. Another situation involves ministry to one in crisis, often a medical crisis. My friend Susan McKinney has battled cancer for several years. A young mother of two boys, she traveled with me and shared her testimony at retreats I attended. She distributed a handout entitled "Do's and Don'ts for the Seriously or Terminally Ill."

Since that time Susan has gone to be with the Lord. I feel confident she would want me to include this material to help you as you minister to those struggling with a traumatic illness or other situation.

Don't

1. Tell the individual how your aunt died from whatever illness she is suffering.

2. Say, "Call me if you need anything" or, "If I can help, call me."

3. Cut off the person if they want to talk about the death, the funeral arrangements, or the person who died.

4. Discourage the ill individual from seeking *legitimate* spiritual counsel even though you personally may not believe it will help. Don't try to put God in a box as to how you think he must think or act. He won't fit.

5. Carelessly quote Romans 8:28. This is a retrospective verse. It takes on meaning for the ill person *after* the illness when they can look back in retrospect. Always include verse 29 with Romans 8:28.

6. Ignore the patient's spouse. It is much easier to be the patient than it is the spouse of the patient.

7. Pull away from people. Don't think, *This person is going to die; therefore, to keep from getting hurt, I will withdraw.*

8. Tell someone you know exactly how she feels if you have not been through a similar experience.

9. Make the patient feel guilty if she is struggling spiritually or cannot seem to pray.

10. Be a discourager.

Do

1. Tell someone how God has healed and can still heal. Be an encourager not a discourager.

2. Anticipate the needs of the family by preparing meals, cleaning the house, including the children of the ill person in activities so their lives can be as normal as possible, and helping with shopping.

3. Listen to their fears and sorrows, even though it may hurt. If the person is terminally ill, encourage her to put her funeral arrangements in writing—decisions about music, preacher, open/closed casket, clothing, and so forth. If there is a particular

item of clothing or jewelry she wants a friend or relative to have, make a list. Give a copy of the arrangements to the pastor and to two close friends so the family does not have to do this.

4. Encourage the individual to pursue and respond to biblical teaching concerning prayer and healing (see James 5:14–15).

5. Quote Scripture that is uplifting and encouraging: Isaiah 41:10; 53:6; 1 Thessalonians 5:18; 1 Peter 2:24.

6. Reach out to the spouse. Invite them to lunch and listen to them talk and cry. Just listen.

7. Go to the ill person and put your arm around her, even if you can't do anything else. Tell her you love her. A hug or an arm around the shoulder goes a long way.

8. Share how the Lord brought you through it if you have been through a similar experience. Explain how it has matured your relationship with him.

9. Encourage the patient to read Psalms. Psalms 46; 23; 27; 62; and 103 are especially meaningful.

10. Be an *encourager.*

In all of these ways, you can extend the love of Jesus and encourage others to do the same. You will be able to say with confidence those words spoken by Paul, "For you know that we dealt with each of you as a father [mother] deals with his [her] children; encouraging, comforting and urging you to live lives worthy of God, who calls you" (1 Thess. 2:11–12).

Benefits are implicit in the following comments made by women who have been recipients or involved in a ministry of caring.

The need to realize I'm not the only one struggling with specific stresses, gaining ideas from older women on how to cope, and encouragement in growth have been the benefits of care group ministry in my life.

Fellowship with other Christian women has met my need for friendship. It has encouraged me as a wife and mother. Fun, food, and fellowship equal encouragement.

Two years ago I was contemplating leaving my husband. Through the caring and instruction I received in our women's Bible study on Ruth, I came to understand my feelings of bitterness. Though no one in the study knew my desperation, Christ used that study to take my hand and help me confess my thoughts and actions to my husband. My husband was shocked; however, through much pain, prayer, confession, and forgiveness, we have rebuilt a marriage through obedience to Christ.

The need to explore my own emotions and troubles with Christian friends has been such an encouragement as answers come from others' similar experiences.

Bearing one another's burdens has been a blessing to me and shown me I'm needed in the body of Christ. I have been made to feel that I am special to the Lord through the caring and attention of other godly women. Certain needs are met by my Christian friends that my husband can't meet because he has a man's perspective.

After my husband left, Phil and Linda began to include me in family activities. Linda began to suggest ways that I could help the church. This caring made me feel a part of the church family. I appreciate being responsible to the church and it to me.

The caring of Christian women gives me the courage to go on when it gets tough. I see how God has worked things out in the lives of others and learn that only he knows what's best for me. Precious sisters in Jesus have shown they care.

Since my husband isn't a Christian, the fellowship of these women is my lifeblood. Spending time with other mothers of young children has helped me handle problems that arise with the wisdom of others' experience.

Warmth, companionship, counseling, encouragement, prayer support, and Christian role modeling has done much to relieve my loneliness.

Two weeks ago I lost my four and one-half-year-old son. The love and support of caring women helped me through this terrible time in my life.

Christian women have ministered to me through difficult times of back problems, surgery, and the loss of a child.

I have felt the strength and comfort given me through the love and caring of Christian women in the loss of my husband.

I am blessed as I visit and share with older women who are shut-ins and with new mothers who have had their first child. I receive as much or more blessing through this ministry as I see how they accept this small token of my love and concern.

My husband and I were told we couldn't have children, but through the prayers of my dear Christian friends and family, we have a daughter. I always had support from them when I was down, and their prayers helped me make it when I had a miscarriage. The example of the life of godly, mature, committed Christian women encourages, inspires, and challenges me.

Won't you ask God how you, too, might bless and be blessed through his ministry of care and encouragement?

Chapter 10

WHAT IS YOUR PLACE
IN MINISTRY?

ELAINE L. STEDMAN wrote in her *Decision* article "God and Today's Woman," "To love each person we meet, laying down our lives, our 'right,' as he laid down his life, his right—caring, reaching out, giving, listening, pouring the oil of his Spirit on troubled waters—this is God's plan for beautiful womanhood: to make Jesus Christ visible."[1]

The power of a woman's influence is great. We see this in the lives of many biblical women: Sarah, Esther, Deborah, Ruth, Priscilla, Dorcas, Lydia, and a host of others.

The potential to become all God created you to be as a woman is the most exciting challenge of life. We were born to image his Son. It is an indescribable privilege and pursuit. "For those God foreknew he also predestined to be conformed to the likeness of his Son" (Rom. 8:29).

Joyce Turner writes, "The moral standard of a society, too, is largely dependent on its women, and history testifies to the great influence that godly mothers and grandmothers have had down through the ages."[2]

A recent survey showed that 75 percent of the questioned twelve through seventeen-year-old students claim their religious beliefs matched those of their mothers. Women often do not realize the impact they have on their families and others around them. It really isn't a matter of choice. You will affect those in your sphere of influence—family, friends, and coworkers—even when you are unaware of doing so. Rather than live on the defensive, trying to fade into the background, why not shine the light of Jesus Christ to those around you?

Jesus said, "Let your light shine before men, that they may see your good deeds and praise your Father in heaven" (Matt. 5:16). Walking with our Lord requires commitment. Shining his light is one of the aspects of commitment that should be our delight and desire.

Jesus did *not* say, "Let your light shine if you have time. Let your light shine when your life is free of problems. Let your light shine when you think you have finally gotten everything under control."

Too many of us create excuses to procrastinate. I've heard women say, "When I finally get organized, I'll manage everything in my office." There is a cost to be counted as one shining God's light. Jesus tells us in Luke 14:33, "Any of you who does not give up everything he has cannot be my disciple." We must be certain that he is the most important person in our lives and his will the most important desire.

As we surrender ourselves totally to him, we will experience the richness of fulfilling his purposes for us that was established before the creation of the world. "For we are God's workmanship, created in Christ Jesus to do good works, which God prepared in advance for us to do" (Eph. 2:10).

Are Christ and his plan more important to you than your own life, schedules, plans, concerns, and organization? Can you trust him to care for you as you seek to be used by him for his glory? He is trustworthy. "Those who know your name will trust in you, for you, LORD, have never forsaken those who seek you" (Ps. 9:10).

Commitment is defined as a pledge or promise to do something. Can you commit yourself now to shine the light of Christ to those around you as he directs you? Don't miss God's opportunity to use you for his glory. Take a moment now and look back at the Personal Inventory Questionnaire in chapter 1. Have you been able to identify more clearly some of the areas in which God may desire to use you?

Reflect on the following questionnaire. Prayerfully consider new ways to draw nearer to God and grow in your understanding of his will and purpose for you.

Personal Growth Inventory

In a notebook or diary list the methods you plan to use to reach the following goals:

1. I will grow in my relationship with God and develop into the woman he wants and expects me to be by the following actions:

- Begin a daily prayer journal.
- Look for and use an inductive Bible study in my daily devotions.

2. I will show Christ's love to my family in the coming days and weeks by taking action to:

- Prepare a candlelight dinner for my husband and myself once a month.
- Have a special family time to share our favorite Scripture and tell one thing we most appreciate about each member.
- Discover unique ways to show my family I love them each week.

3. I will make every effort to identify everyone I need to forgive or ask forgiveness as found in Matthew 18:15.

4. I will concentrate on using my former unrecognized talents or gifts that the Lord has identified through reading this book.

5. I will pray for people whom he has revealed to me as ones I need to pray for and consider ministering to them in the near future.

6. I will consider the ministries listed in this book that caught my interest.

7. I will pray for God's will in regard to these ministries.

8. I will map a goal to implement my plans according to God's leading.

9. I will identify people I know who might be hurting and reach out to them to copy Christ's love in a tangible way.

10. I will consult my list each day and follow up on the book's suggestions by _____.

How can you know the will of God for you as you seek to minister in his name? Through many years in ministry, God has taught me significant truths. As I consider his place in ministry for me, I realize that I will not be able to meet every need I see. Leaving many untouched and untaught, Jesus was able to say at the end of his life, "[Father,] I have brought you glory on earth by completing the work you gave me to do" (John 17:4). As we seek to know the Father's will, many will go untouched and untaught in our lives, but if we obey his direction, at the end of our lives we will be able to say with Jesus, "Father, I have completed the work that you gave me to do."

I also learned an invaluable lesson through the sermon of a New England preacher. He explained why it is so important to know the will of God for our service and to do only that which is ours to do. If we are in the will of God, there will be joy and fulfillment. But if we are out of the will of God having said yes to a responsibility that is not ours to fulfill, we will not only experience the sorrow of being outside God's will but will rob someone else of their place in his work and ministry.

After speaking at a conference, I developed the following Life Activity Worksheet in response to women seeking help to determine God's will for ministry. Take time to fill in this sheet and consider it carefully.

Life Activity Worksheet

1. For one week list all your activities. Include those activities often taken for granted but which comprise a significant

investment of time and talent (menu development, grocery shopping, laundry, cooking). These are important and need to be seen as integral to your schedule since an evaluation of your free time can only be calculated after these tasks are incorporated into your time schedule.

2. Evaluate each of these activities carefully to determine whether it is God's will for your time. To do this apply the following four categories to help in your evaluation:

Scriptural insight (Ps. 119:105)–Is this activity consistent with God's Word and his direction to you in light of his Word?

God-orchestrated circumstances (Jer. 29:11)–Can you see God's hand in orchestrating the circumstances of your life to confirm that this activity is according to his will and able to be accomplished by his power in the time you are allotted?

Counsel of believers (Prov. 15:22)–Do you have Christian friends who can offer insight as you seek to know if a particular task or responsibility is according to God's will for your life? Though no one else can determine the will of God for you, a trusted Christian friend may be able to offer advice and insight that will either confirm or negate a particular activity as God's will for you.

Duplication factor (Eph. 4:11)–If after running all activities through the grid of these first three determinants you find yourself still uncertain about your priorities and the use of your time, you might ask yourself if there are activities that others are fully capable of or more capable of fulfilling than you. For example, in my life, I was trained as a child to become a concert pianist. Though I chose not to pursue this career, I often played the piano for my church. When particularly overwhelmed as a mother of three, while seeking to know God's will for my time and talent, it became clear that he desired that I speak and write. How could I find the time?

I soon realized there was a young woman in our church who was fully capable of serving as church accompanist. It was the special gift God had given her, and in essence I was robbing her of her place in the will of God while I filled the position. As soon as I realized that giving up that responsibility would provide the hours I needed to speak and write, it quickly became clear God's plan for me was to speak and write, not play the organ. As a result I resigned the position, and she accepted it. Both of us were delighted as we began to realize God's joy in experiencing his will and purpose unfold in our lives.

Activities	Scriptural Insights	God-Orchestrated Circumstances	Counsel of Believers	Duplication Factor

3. Write phrases you learn from the following passages that strengthen your ability to trust God as you seek to know his will.

Psalm 94:16–19

Hebrews 4:14–16

Isaiah 25:4–5, 9

Psalm 116

Psalm 13:5–6

Psalm 52:8–9

4. According to Galatians 3:1–3; John 15:5; and Romans 8:11, by whose power are you to perform every action of life?

5. Write a prayer to God asking for his insight and power to say no to those requests, demands, and activities he has not initiated (though they may seem good) that are instead keeping you from his best. You can then say yes to him and his plans for your life.

As you continue to consider God's ministry plans for you, always remember that we are to reflect his glory. John Piper defines the glory of God in his book *Desiring God* in the following words: "God's glory is the beauty of His manifold perfections. It can refer to the bright and awesome radiance that sometimes breaks forth in visible manifestations. Or it can refer to the infinite moral excellence of character. In either case it signifies a reality of infinite greatness and worth."[3]

We are told that we can behold his glory and have the privilege of reflecting it. In 2 Corinthians 4:7–10, Paul assures us, "We have this treasure in jars of clay to show that this all-surpassing power is from God and not from us. We are hard pressed on every side, but not crushed; perplexed, but not in despair; persecuted, but not abandoned; struck down, but not destroyed. We always carry around in our body the death of Jesus, so that the life of Jesus may also be revealed in our body."

Stop and commit your life afresh to Jesus Christ as Lord. Ask him to use you for his exact purposes to reach the world around you for him. Write a prayer of commitment and thank him for his plan that includes you.

Beth Mainhood in her book *Reaching Your World* writes, "Obedience to God brings freedom. The defiant enemy propagates the false message that freedom is self-expression. But when we obey God and help fulfill his Great Commission to the world, we have freedom in its truest sense."[4]

She goes on to say that this freedom "disallows the claims of self-centeredness."[5] It is a fact we clamor for respect, attention, and rights. "But it is in giving that we receive, when the giving is to Christ. This rewarded freedom to give allows us to die in order to bring forth many new lives."[6]

In giving, we receive. Jesus guarantees it. "Give, and it will be given to you. A good measure, pressed down, shaken together and running over, will be poured into your lap" (Luke 6:38). The measure you use—faith, time, talents, gifts—will be credited to you.

Won't you begin today? The opportunity is yours!

NOTES

Chapter 1

1. Lorine Shannon, *Lord, What Do You Want Me to Do?*, manual, 2.

2. Gigi Tchividjian, *Diapers and Dishes or Pinstripes and Pumps* (Nashville: Thomas Nelson, 1987), 35.

3. Joyce Turner, "Women Can Make a Vital Impact on Society," *Church Disciple*, Aug. 1987.

4. Cole Huffman, "Meet Your Cell Mates," *Discipleship Journal*, March/April, 2004, 54.

Chapter 2

1. Evelyn Christianson, *What Happens When People Pray* (Wheaton, Ill.: Victor Books, 1975), 13.

2. J. Oswald Sanders, *Prayer Power Unlimited* (Chicago: Moody Bible Institute, 1977), 120.

3. Rosalind Rinker, *Prayer: Conversing with God* (Grand Rapids, Mich.: Zondervan, 1959), 42–43.

4. Ray A. Stedman, *Talking to My Father* (Portland, Oreg.: Multnomah Press, 1975), 106.

Chapter 3

1. Susan Hunt, "Reach Out and Comfort Someone," *The Wick*, Fall 1988.

2. Ralph Wilson, "The Value of a Caring Community," *Decision*, October 1989, 25–26.

3. Dee Brestin, *The Friendship of Women* (Wheaton, Ill.: Victor Books, 1988), 152.

4. Lucibel Van Atta, *Women Encouraging Women* (Portland, Oreg.: Multnomah Press, 1987), 28.

5. Ibid., 144.

6. Beth Mainhood, *Reaching Your World* (Colorado Springs, Colo.: Navpress, 1986), 68.

Chapter 4

1. Aristides, *The PCA Messenger,* Nov. 1989, cover page.

2. Ruth Senter, "Invader in the Sanctuary," *Partnership,* January/February 1987, 4.

3. June Curtis, "A Plate of Warm Cookies," *Virtue,* Dec. 1985, 34.

4. Barbara Barker, "Retreat Reflections," *South Texas Presbyterian WIC News,* Feb. 1988.

5. John Ragland, *South Texas Presbyterian WIC News,* July 1987.

6. Frank Barker, "Retreat Reflections," *South Texas Presbyterian WIC News,* Feb. 1988.

7. Martha Chamberlain, "Breaking Bread with the World," *Partnership,* March/April 1986, 42.

Chapter 6

1. Anne Marley Work, "Tell It Often, Tell It Well," *Worldwide Challenge,* March/April 1988, 29.

2. Dave Swartz, "There Is No Plan "B," *Decision,* February 1989, 17.

3. George Barna, *Think Like Jesus* (Brentwood, Tenn.: Integrity Publishers, 2003).

4. Mark Littleton, "Plant Seeds, Not Burning Bushes," *Discipleship Journal* 25 (1985), 37.

5. Ibid.

6. Anna Marie Larkins, "Evangelism on the Job," *Worldwide Challenge,* Feb. 1987, 62.

7. Glenn Plate, "Sharing 9 to 5," *Worldwide Challenge,* Feb. 1987, 58.

8. Swartz, 17.

9. Pete Hammond, "On-the-Job Witnessing the WORKS," *Christian Herald,* Oct. 1988, 18.

10. Bill Bright, "Searching for that Missing Joy?" *Worldwide Challenge,* Feb. 1988, 10.

11. Bonnie Bruno, "Guaranteed to Bloom," *Virtue*, May/June 1987, 59.

12. Plate, 59.

13. Gladys Hunt, *"How to" Handbook for Inductive Bible Study Leaders* (Wheaton, Ill.: Harold Shaw, 1971), 22.

Chapter 7

1. William J. Brown, "Experiencing God's Heart for the City," *Decision*, June 1989, 29.

2. Dewey Davidson, "Pastor's Goal to Reach the 'Common Joe,'" *Greenville Herald Banner*, January 10, 1987, A-4.

3. Patricia Hershey, "And How Shall They Hear . . . Without a Letter," *World Vision*, April 1977, 16.

Chapter 8

1. Susan Hunt, "Reach Out and Comfort Someone," *The WICK*, Summer 1988.

2. Morton Hunt, "When Everyday Stress Turns Serious," *Family Circle*, September 1989, 52.

3. Becky Foster Still, "Married, No Children," *Focus on the Family*, April 1989, 2–4.

4. Ibid.

5. Fran Sandin, "10 Ways to Say 'I Care,'" *Evangelical Beacon*, April 1989, 4–5.

6. Susan Hunt, "Reach Out and Comfort Someone," *The WICK*, Fall 1988.

Chapter 9

1. Mark A. Taylor, "Why Community?" *The Lookout*, May 1987, 12.

2. Lucinda McDowell, "You Can Be an Encourager," *Woman's Touch*, January/February 1989, 6.

Chapter 10

1. Elaine L. Stedman, "God and Today's Woman," *Decision*, 1971.

2. Joyce Turner, "Women Can Make a Vital Impact on Society," *Church Disciple 1:1* (August 1987).

3. John Piper, *Desiring God* (Portland, Oreg.: Multnomah Press, 1986), 31.

4. Beth Mainhood, *Reaching Your World* (Colorado Springs, Colo.: Navpress, 1986), 109.

5. Ibid.

6. Ibid.